P9-CAO-182

CHIPS

CHIPS

Reinventing A Favorite Food

Chris Bryant

An Imprint of Sterling Publishing
387 Park Avenue South
New York, NY 10016

Text © 2014 by Chris Bryant
Photography © 2014 by Lark Books, an Imprint of Sterling Publishing Co., Inc.
Photography, right column, page 17 © 2014 Chris Bryant

All rights reserved. No part of this publication may be reproduced, stored in a
retrieval system, or transmitted, in any form or by any means (including electronic, mechanical,
photocopying, recording, or otherwise) without prior written permission from the publisher.

ISBN 978-1-4547-0850-6

Library of Congress Cataloging-in-Publication Data

Bryant, Chris, 1961-
  Chips / Chris Bryant.
    pages cm
  Summary: "Making homemade chips from fruits, cheese, meat, tortillas, and
vegetables by drying, frying, and baking"-- provided by publisher.
  Includes index.
  ISBN 978-1-4547-0850-6
  1. Snack foods. 2. Dried foods. 3. Fried food. 4. Baked products. I. Title.
  TX740.B6526 2014
  641.5'3--dc23
                              2013043169

Distributed in Canada by Sterling Publishing
c/o Canadian Manda Group, 165 Dufferin Street
Toronto, Ontario, Canada M6K 3H6
Distributed in the United Kingdom by GMC Distribution Services
Castle Place, 166 High Street, Lewes, East Sussex, England BN7 1XU
Distributed in Australia by Capricorn Link (Australia) Pty. Ltd.
P.O. Box 704, Windsor, NSW 2756, Australia

For information about custom editions, special sales, and premium and corporate purchases,
please contact Sterling Special Sales at 800-805-5489 or specialsales@sterlingpublishing.com.

Email academic@larkbooks.com for information about desk and examination copies.
The complete policy can be found at larkcrafts.com.

Every effort has been made to ensure that all the information in this book is accurate.
However, due to differing conditions, tools, and individual skills, the publisher cannot be responsible
for any injuries, losses, and other damages that may result from the use of the information in this book.

Manufactured in China

2 4 6 8 10 9 7 5 3 1

larkcrafts.com

CHIP MAKING BASICS

POTATO

VEGGIE

INTRODUCTION

No doubt about it, chips are A number 1, the king of American snacks. Compact, concentrated wafers of joy, they can be consumed easily (on the couch, in the car, in the park, on the beach) and found just about anywhere, from gas stations to grocery stores. Chips are ubiquitous and delicious, a culinary classic. Why, then, do we delegate their preparation to the processed-food industry? The DIY spirit inspires folks to make their own pickles, cheeses, and beer (and sausages, jellies, breads, and pastas), so why not add chips to the list?

I say it's time to bring chip-making home. The process is simple, and it has instant-gratification results. Plus—a big plus—you get to be in charge of quality control. You can make chips from healthy, wholesome ingredients using the best oils, and you can season them with the things you like. Forget about the unpronounceable additives and preservatives that come with store-bought chips.

One of the best things about making chips at home is that it allows you to take into account the seasonality and locality of ingredients. The best beet chips are made from local beet varieties available at farmers' markets. When zucchinis are proverbially "running out of your ears," that's the time to dispatch them as garden-fresh chips. And the tastiest potato chips you can ever hope to eat come from spuds that are fresh from the ground.

Another bonus: Homemade chips are supremely economical. Industrially made chips cost 100 to 1000 times more than the raw ingredients inside the air-filled bag—think about that when you grab a $3.00 sack of potato chips with 15 cents' worth of spuds inside.

Chip-making is also lots of fun! It's a process akin to alchemy: you combine a raw material with some basic ingredients, follow a formula, and come out the other side with an eye-rollingly delicious snack. Your family and friends will be completely impressed when you pass around freshly made kale chips, apple chips, or prosciutto chips—bites you conjured up in your own kitchen. Delicious, easy magic!

This book starts out with the chip-making basics—all the info you need regarding tools, materials (not many at all!), and ingredients (basically, oil, salt, and seasonings). Then it's on to the techniques section, where you'll learn about cooking chips. The focus here is on the three basic ways chips are produced—by frying, baking, or dehydrating. There's nothing complicated about these techniques, and there's a bonus—a photo chart that documents each process step by step.

Next up, and for the rest of the book, are the chip recipes. You'll find a myriad of flavors and savors and discover that chips can be made from all the food categories—roots, plants, fruits, proteins, and grains. Some of the recipes produce spicy hot or exotically seasoned chips. Others will give you sweet, dessert morsels. And plenty of them result in good, old salty chips, just the way you like them. To kick up the chip-eating experience, I've included recipes for scrumptious dips, drizzles, and over-the-top toppings—a feast of flavors and loads of ideas to inspire you in your own chipping adventure.

It's time to bid the snack aisle good-bye and start making your own chips! So pick out some recipes, gather your tools, and get chipping—and go ahead, call them Artisan Chips, because that's what they are.

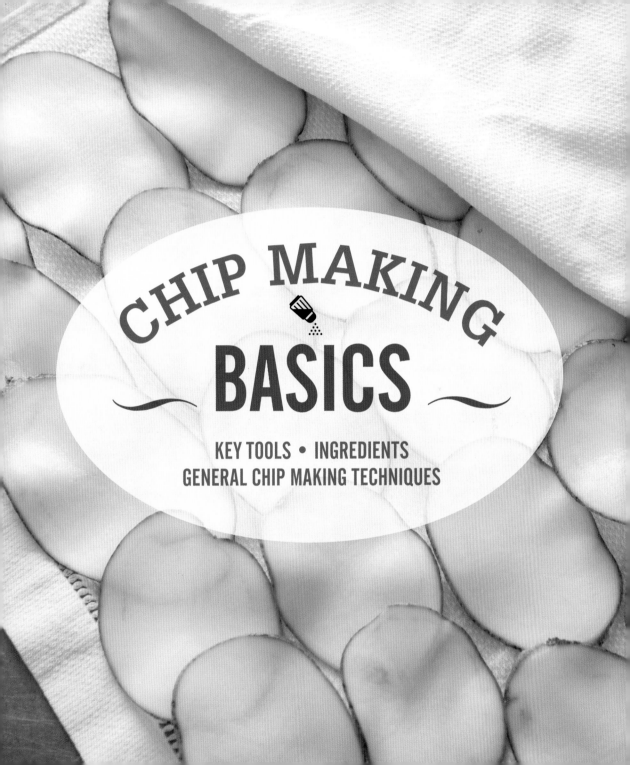

CHIP MAKING
BASICS

KEY TOOLS • INGREDIENTS
GENERAL CHIP MAKING TECHNIQUES

KEY TOOLS

FOR PREP

KNIVES

To make the chips in this book, two good knives are all you need—a Little One and a Big One. The Little One is for snipping off the ends of things and carving in and out of tight curves. I'm sure you already have a trusty paring knife. Sharpen it, then check it off the list.

The next knife up is the Big One. If you're cutting chips by hand, this one's important to get right. You need a very sharp knife with a wide blade. The words "very sharp" cannot be stressed enough. Making chips is all about cutting food into thin, uniform slices. A kind-of/sort-of sharp knife isn't going to cut it. There are technical, safety, and even molecular reasons to ditch a dull knife, but I'll spare you the explanation. The other important factor to consider is blade size. A wide blade stays in contact with the food as it travels downward, creating a sort of guide to keep the knife straight.

If there's more than one chef's knife in the drawer, go for the one with the thinnest, lightest blade. Sharpen it! Then make some practice cuts with a potato. If the knife doesn't work for you, test others until you find one that yields chip-worthy results. My go-to knife is a Kiwi brand Thai chef's knife that I picked up for under $10 at an Asian market. Its thin rectangular blade quickly sharpens to a razor's edge with a couple of swipes across a sharpening steel.

MANDOLINE

I'll just come right out and say it: Nothing beats the uniformity and predictability of chips cut with a mandoline. A mandoline-cut chip cooks evenly, with no thin, overcooked edges or thick, under-cooked ends. If you really enjoy making chips, consider procuring a mandoline.

Once an intimidating and expensive piece of equipment associated with mustachioed chefs in puffy hats, the mandoline is now a mainstream gadget with user-friendly designs and budget-friendly prices—some fall in the $15 range.

Mandoline mechanics are simple: You adjust the blade housed in the base to the exact chip thickness you like and slide your food back and forth across it. The chips fall away in amazing uniformity, and the process is remarkably fast—and satisfying.

The Japanese Benriner (*bneri* means useful in Japanese) brand of mandoline is a favorite of chefs and home cooks alike. Its screw-set blade adjusts to paper-thin, it's easy to clean, and it stores flat. OXO makes a couple of nifty, simple-to-use models with durable ceramic blades. A trip to a well-stocked Asian market should turn up some interesting and inexpensive options.

CUT-RESISTANT GLOVES

Going hand in hand with a mandoline are cut-resistant gloves, a small kitchen investment that makes cutting close to the mandoline blade safer. Some gloves are composed of metal chainmail and nothing more, while others are higher tech, made of knitted stainless-steel thread that's been coated with nylon or polyester. As the name implies, cut-resistant gloves are not fail-safe. You should cut chips using the mandoline's cutting guard once you get close to the end of anything you're cutting.

FOOD PROCESSOR

If you have a food processor with cutting blades, you might be able to use it for making chips. It depends on how thick the blade cuts. Many Cuisinart® and KitchenAid® models come with 2 mm blades, an ideal size that's just a smidgeon thicker than the $1/16$ inch- (or about 1.6 mm) thick slices recommended in many of the recipes. Other models feature adjustable blades that can be set with the turn of a screw.

Clockwise from top-right ① table-top mandoline ② cut-resistant glove ③ kitchen towel ④ y-shaped peeler ⑤ chef's knife ⑥ paring knife ⑦ Thai chef's knife ⑧ food processor blades ⑨ hand-held mandoline

The processor's feed tube is another decisive factor. It should be large enough to accommodate whatever you're cutting. Most full-sized processors have tubes large enough for a potato to pass through with little or no trimming. Choose produce that fits the feed tube whenever possible.

VEGETABLE PEELER

The standard side-blade peeler is designed for long vegetables like carrots. Cut away from yourself and the peels fly. Fun. For round produce, I'm a fan of the yoke-shaped vegetable peeler—or Y-peeler. The one I use has a wide plastic handle that feels good to grasp. Because it's easy to apply even pressure, you can use a Y-peeler to cut chips from slender vegetables such as carrots, or produce that's been trimmed to match blade width.

KITCHEN TOWELS

Many of the recipes instruct you to soak starchy vegetable slices in water, then drain and roll them in a kitchen towel to dry before frying. You can use a linen tea towel, cotton flour-sack towel, or terrycloth towel—any kind will work as long as it's clean and dry. Avoid using anything that's been washed in strongly perfumed laundry detergent unless you're going for a springtime-fresh chip.

FOR FRYING

THERMOMETER

There are four types of frying thermometers, all of which can be purchased inexpensively. Make sure the one you get registers up to 400°F and has a sturdy, tight clip so that it can be attached to a frying vessel.

Glass-tube thermometers have been around for a century and is still an excellent instrument. If you use this kind, make sure the clip cuff fits tightly around the cylinder so the thermometer can't slip to the bottom of the pot and give a misreading or break. Because only its bottom bulb needs to be submerged, a glass-tube thermometer is a good choice for frying in shallow oil.

Ruler-style thermometers are designed with a thermometer housed in a flat metal case. Most models have sturdy adjustable clips and heatproof handles. The bulb is held in place above the base so the thermometer can sit securely on the bottom of the pot. Avoid brands with loose thermometer tubes—these can slip out of position and give inaccurate readings.

Digital thermometers are a fantastic instrument that provides an immediate reading. Some models have large, easy-to-view readouts. No longer an expensive gizmo for pros and show-offs, a good digital thermometer can be had for under $20. For frying, I prefer an all-in-one model to a two-part model—having a wire running from the cooktop to connect the sensor and readout doesn't seem like a good idea.

Dial-gauge thermometers are an inexpensive and popular gadget. But most models specify that the stem be submerged in 2 inches of liquid. Add those 2 inches to the 1/4-inch clearance from the bottom, and you may end up using more oil than necessary. That said, some models—particularly instant-read gauges—can measure at shallow depths, and some give accurate readings even while specifying 2-inch immersion. I like dial-gauge thermometers because they show me visually when I'm in The Zone for frying.

WIRE COOLING RACKS

All of the frying recipes require that you set up a draining station by placing a wire rack upside down over absorbent paper on a baking sheet. The wire rack should span most of a flat baking sheet or fit inside a rimmed one. You'll also use wire racks to cool chips and drain fried chips.

PAPER TOWELS, PAPER BAGS, NEWSPAPER

You need clean, absorbent paper for draining chips. Choose the type that suits you, spread it on a baking sheet or pan, and cover it with an upturned wire cooling rack.

① digital thermometer
② glass-tube thermometer
③ ruler-style thermometer
④ spider ⑤ strainer
⑥ slotted spoon
⑦ cooling racks
⑧ paper towels

SLOTTED SPOON

The classic oval slotted spoon (you probably have one in your kitchen drawer) will do fine for stirring, turning, and scooping chips. Variations on this common utensil abound. A spoon with a long handle and a round metal end, either with wide slots or open-wire mesh, is especially well suited for tending chips as they cook and for lifting them out of the oil.

SPIDER

This wide, lightweight spoon-meets-strainer is the ideal frying tool. It has a shallow metal basket, usually with a woven pattern that resembles a spider's web. Asian-made spiders often have bamboo handles, while other types are sleek and industrial. The spider's wide scoop and open weave make it a helpful tool for lowering food into oil, and nothing beats the speed and efficiency of a spider when it comes to scooping up finished chips—an important consideration, since they can go from perfect to burned in seconds.

STRAINER

A mesh strainer is heavier than a spider, and typically less porous. When you transfer chips out of a pot with a strainer, you'll find that it holds onto oil for a few extra seconds. Still, you can move a lot of chips in one scoop with a strainer, so it's a good tool to have in your arsenal if you don't have a spider.

FRYING VESSELS
A wide, heavy pot

Most of the frying recipes in this book call for a wide, heavy pot. Why is that important? Wide is helpful because in most cases, chips are fried in a single layer, and a wide surface area accommodates more chips at a time without crowding the pot. Heavy is important because the mass of the pot will hold and distribute heat without dramatic drops and spikes in temperature. A weighty pot also sits safely and solidly on the burner, preventing the hot oil from easily being jarred and splashed.

The ideal frying pot is a Dutch oven made of cast iron. The heavy, thick bottom and sides of a Dutch oven make it superior for holding heat, affording the maximum amount of cushion when cold food goes into the oil. High sides provide ample headspace and room to clip on a thermometer.

Enamel-coated cast-iron pots and Dutch ovens, such as those made by Le Creuset®, are first-rate. The smooth enamel coating makes them easy to clean and non-reactive. However, a stainless steel, clad-style pot is fine for frying if it has a heavy bottom.

Deep pots, particularly stockpots, are not recommended for frying. The sides are too high for clipping on the thermometer and, in order to turn and move the chips, your hand would have to hover directly above the oil, in the line of hot steam.

Skillets

For shallow oil cooking you can use a 10- or 12-inch skillet, preferably one made of cast iron. Bear in mind that most skillets are only 2 inches deep, so in order to maintain a safe headspace, you'll need to keep the oil depth between 3/4 and 1 inch. A deep cast-iron skillet, sometimes called a chicken fryer, is an ideal chip cooker—with 3-inch sides, it's second only to a Dutch oven. Stainless steel, clad-style French skillets have higher sides than regular skillets, making them a good choice for chip frying too.

Woks

The angled sides and bowl shape of a wok create both a wide surface and a deep well for oil, and the wide margin around the oil means less splattering on your stove and counters. A little oil in a wok performs like a much larger pot of oil. I do most of my frying in a wok. It's important to have a stable set-up when using a wok for frying. Don't use a flimsy one on a precariously positioned stand. Use a heavy wok—the cast-iron kind is ideal—and preferably one with a flat bottom.

Electric fryers

Full disclosure: I do not own a deep-fat fryer, or what's more delicately referred to as an electric fryer. For me, the temptation of having a font of oil always at the ready for spur-of-the-moment frying binges is too great. But a fryer is definitely handy. Its drop-down, lift-out basket is a huge time-saver for chip frying because your batches can be larger. Today's fryers offer digital readouts, charcoal-filtration odor control, and circulating oil filtration to keep oil fresher for longer. Another plus: Oil can be stored and reused in an electric fryer, so it's always there for you, always ready...

Electric fry pans and kettle cookers

Two different versions of the same idea, these appliances are essentially electric burners attached to skillets or pots. If you already own one and like to use it, you might enjoy making chips with it. Most kettles come with lift-out baskets, and most electric skillets have high sides—a plus for shallow frying. Although there's a thermostat on the plug housing, it only shows whether or not you've reached a certain temperature. You'll still need an external thermometer. The majority of these products have plastic, polymer-based non-stick surfaces—something to consider if you dislike that type of surface.

FOR BAKING

BAKING SHEETS

I probably don't need to tell you this, but here goes: Baking sheets are flat, and rimmed baking sheets have sides. For most purposes, the two types can be used interchangeably. I make a distinction in the recipes only when you need sides to corral chips that might roll or slide while going in and out of the oven, or when something has the potential to ooze off the sides.

Some recipes instruct you to sandwich chips between two baking sheets (or pans) and weigh the top one down so that the chips stay flat and cook evenly. If your baking pans (or sheets) are a miss-matched collection that you've assembled over time, you might need to puzzle out the pairings before diving into one of these recipes.

PARCHMENT PAPER

To create a non-stick surface that doesn't require a coating of oil, line baking sheets with parchment paper. I love parchment paper—it's my go-to pan liner. It comes in rolls or precut sheets that are typically 9 x 13 inches, the size of most baking sheets. Parchment paper can be reused until it becomes too puckered or too brittle. Don't substitute waxed paper for parchment—they're not the same. The paraffin in waxed paper will smoke and melt. And your chips will taste like crayons.

SILICONE BAKING MATS

These are superior baking-sheet liners. Food simply doesn't stick to them, and delicate things can easily be lifted off—there's no prying involved. Made of fiberglass-reinforced silicone, they're more stick-proof than parchment paper. Mats made by the French brand Silpat® are easy to find, and other brands are available. A word of warning: The mats aren't cheap—they're usually priced in the $10 to $20 range. But they're a good investment. Considering the fact that they can survive about 3,000 trips into the oven, they definitely win out over parchment paper in that respect.

KITCHEN TONGS

Tongs are essential for turning chips mid-way through cooking and for reaching into the oven to fish out single chips that get done early. You may decide to use tongs as a frying tool too, but bear in mind that it takes a few extra seconds to move large batches of cooked chips out of the oil with tongs, and those extra seconds can be critical. For both purposes, use long-handle tongs with an insulated handle.

FOR DEHYDRATING

DEHYDRATOR

There's no denying that this is a large and specialized piece of equipment. I don't recommend purchasing one just because you want to make chips—unless you've already been considering it. If you do own one, hopefully this will inspire you to dig it out of storage. I did, and I think I discovered its highest calling: nacho-cheese kale chips (see page 88).

Advanced dehydrators come equipped with timers and temperature controls measured between 85°F and 155°F. Less complex models only have high, medium, and low settings, or just on and off. In box-style units, such as those made by Excalibur® (which I used for these recipes), the food is stored on drawer-style, pull-out trays. Heat from the back of the dehydrator circulates evenly across all of the trays. Stack-style machines blow heat from the bottom, making it necessary to rearrange the trays during cooking.

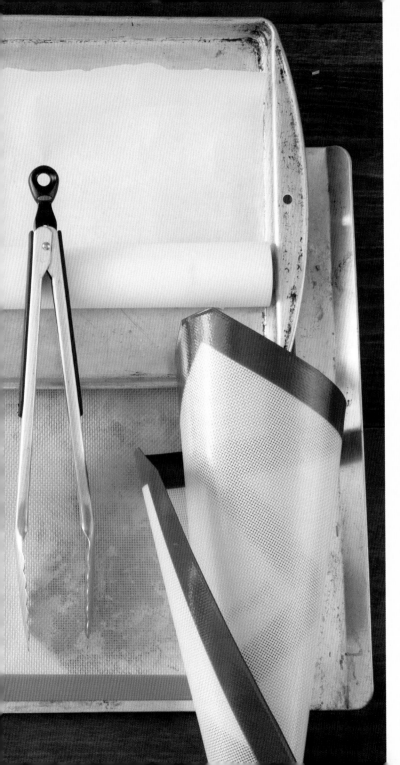

Parchment Wrangling

Parchment paper comes on rolls, which means that when you tear a piece off, it lands on the baking sheet in a tight tube. Trying to make this tube lie flat can be like a scene from a Charlie Chaplin movie. I have a simple trick that solves this problem: Wad the paper up. That's right—tear off a piece, wad it into a tight ball, and spread it out. You've shown it who's boss.

INGREDIENTS

OILS

OILS FOR FRYING

The ideal frying oil has a neutral flavor and a high smoke point (see About Smoke Points). Inexpensive refined vegetable oils such as canola, corn, safflower, sunflower, peanut, and vegetable-oil blends are all formulated for high-temperature frying.

Peanut oil is highly regarded among professional and other ardent fryers as a superior frying oil. I find that peanut oil breaks down slower and doesn't taste "old" as quickly as other vegetable oils, likely because its 450°F smoke point slows down deterioration.

Extra-light olive oil has a slightly higher smoke point than peanut oil, making it very stable. It's considered one of the healthier oils for frying. However, it's a bit more costly and not as easily sourced in large quantities as the other frying oils.

Avocado oil is the holy grail of cooking oil, with a smoke point of 520°F. Given its outstanding healthfulness—many nutritionists believe avocado oil is a superfood—it seems like a no-brainer to pick up a quart and feel absolved of any deep-frying guilt you may harbor. But it's not widely available, and it's also fairly expensive.

Canola oil is among the least expensive and most popular of vegetable oils. I've long been a fan of it thanks to its neutral flavor and attractive price. These days, however, I'm not so enthusiastic. The more I fry with it, the more I notice its early burnout. After about three batches, canola oil tends to turn amber and generate the heavy scent of a greasy-spoon diner. That said, if you aren't a frequent fryer, canola oil would probably work just fine for a batch or two of chips.

Lard and **tallow** are non-grain, non-seed options for frying. Lard comes from pork, while tallow comes from beef. Both were once primary frying oils until they were relegated to the unhealthy column. Today, some contend that oils rendered from pasture-raised, grass-fed pigs and cows are actually healthier than vegetable oils. Time will tell. I do know they're flavorful, and that many folks swear that McDonald's® fries have never been the same since they stopped frying them in beef fat.

CONCERNS ABOUT FRYING OILS

Discussion abounds about the bad things that happen to certain oils at high temperatures. Compelling arguments can be made against using practically every one of the common vegetable frying oils—concerns about GMOs, the release of free radicals, and the noxious chemicals used to process some oils. If you discover a passion for frying chips, and you're keen to compare the pros and cons of cooking oils, I recommend checking out the latest research online. You'll find tons of up-to-date information that can help you choose an oil you're comfortable with (or, just as important, identify the ones to avoid).

FLAVORFUL FATS

Bacon drippings, chicken fat, and duck fat possess so much luscious flavor that they can be qualified as seasonings. Try replacing the oil in the baked-chips recipes with one of these. Chicken and duck fat give a savory roasted taste to root chips, and just a little rendered bacon grease packs full-on bacon flavor. When used for frying, these fats will send your chips right over the top. This is especially true of duck fat. This super-deluxe oil is acclaimed for what it does for fries and chips. For out more about sourcing and using these fabulous fats, see Pan-Fried Decadence on page 49.

USING AND REUSING FRYING OIL

Don't worry about dumping an entire bottle of oil into your pot—you can use it again and again. Many chefs and fried-food aficionados believe that fresh oil is just plain blah, and that the ideal flavor plateau for an oil comes with its second or third time on the flame. Some restaurants even add a portion of old oil back into the new when changing out batches! I think there's something to that. When I used veteran oil for these recipes, the chips just tasted better.

So how many times can you reuse oil? It depends on the oil and how you handle it. Oils with higher smoke points hold up to high temperatures longer than oils on the lower end of the scale (see About Smoke Points). If you aim to reuse your oil, choose one with the highest smoke point for your budget and keep it clean. Here are some suggestions that will help you get at least five (and possibly more) uses from a quality oil:

DON'T OVERHEAT: Keep constant tabs on your oil temperature. Except for a few recipes in this book, you should keep your oil from creeping much past 375°F, the high end of deep-frying temperatures.

KEEP IT CLEAN: After each use, as soon as the oil returns to room temperature, strain it. You can use cheesecloth, a fine mesh strainer, or a reusable

About Smoke Points

The temperature at which smoke rises from oil is known as its smoke point. And just as steam rises from water before it boils, smoke rises from oil as it nears its boiling point. The fumes that result are thought to be unhealthy, and they indicate that the oil is breaking down—diminishing in flavor, color, and lifespan. Most vegetable cooking oils are formulated to withstand high frying temperatures. The smoke points of some cooking oils used for frying are listed below.

Most commonly used oils

SAFFLOWER OIL	510°F
CANOLA OIL, HIGH OLEIC	475°F
SOYBEAN OIL, REFINED	460°F
CORN OIL	450°F
PEANUT OIL	450°F
SUNFLOWER OIL, REFINED	440°F
COTTONSEED OIL	420°F
CANOLA OIL, EXPELLER PRESSED	400°F

Less common oils

AVOCADO OIL, REFINED	520°F
OLIVE OIL, EXTRA LIGHT	465°F
COCONUT OIL	450°F
HAZELNUT OIL	430°F
OLIVE OIL, REFINED	430°F
GRAPESEED OIL	420°F
TALLOW (BEEF FAT)	420°F
OLIVE OIL, VIRGIN	410°F
OLIVE OIL, EXTRA VIRGIN	375°F
LARD (PORK FAT)	370°F

Oils not often used

MUSTARD OIL	490°F
RICE BRAN OIL	490°F
PALM OIL	450°F
ALMOND OIL	420°F
GHEE (CLARIFIED BUTTER)	410°F
SESAME OIL	410°F

coffee filter for straining. While frying, use a spoon or small strainer to scoop out any solids that are left behind between batches.

STORE CAREFULLY: Pour cooled, filtered oil back into its original bottle or an airtight glass or metal container. Store the oil in a cool, dark place like the refrigerator or freezer. If you expect to fry again within a day or two, you can store the oil at room temperature unless the weather is really hot.

MONITOR QUALITY: As oil deteriorates, it becomes darker and thicker than fresh oil. While it starts out as nearly odorless, it picks up various undertones (think delicious French fries) along the way. When does that "character" go too far? It's a matter of taste, and you'll know when you smell it.

DISPOSAL: Okay, so this tip isn't about reuse, but it is important. When it comes time to dump your oil, DO NOT—I repeat, do NOT—pour it down the drain, not even with a detergent and hot-water chaser. Used cooking oil wreaks havoc when it coagulates against cool pipes in your house and in your neighborhood. When disposal time rolls around, I return my oil to its original bottle and toss it in the trash.

SEASONINGS

SALTS

The supreme chip seasoning is salt. It's elemental. (Just try to imagine a saltless chip. It can't be done!) Lately there's been a salt surge, with lots of interesting textures and flavors imported from exotic-sounding places—Celtic sea salt, *fleur de sel*, Hawaiian black sea salt. No doubt they're special and unique, and maybe you've found some favorites. But in my recipes I rarely refer to any type by name. Texture is important, however. When I think it matters, I specify kosher salt, fine salt, and coarse salt.

Fine salt is the grind to use when you want evenly distributed, go-deep saltiness with some visible grains. Use table salt or fine sea salt. Powdery ultra-fine salt, sometimes called popcorn salt, coats chips with a fine dusting of concentrated saltiness. A little goes a long way, so be careful not to overdo it. Fine and ultra-fine salts are the best choices to add to seasoning blends because they meld with other ingredients and bind flavors together.

Kosher salt is a specific term I use in the recipes for any flake salt. Moderately coarse grained, kosher salt has a nice presence—you can see the flakes—but it's still fine enough to get into cracks and crevices. The interesting thing about flake salt is how the jagged crystals draw in oil and lock onto chips. Yum. Use any brand of kosher salt or a flake sea salt, such as Maldon.®

Coarse salt is not a blend-into-the-background wallflower. The chunky grains offer individual and intense explosions of flavor—and sound. This is the place to show off colorful or flavorful salts such as Hawaiian red sea salt, briny French grey sea salt, or Himalayan pink rock salt. Coarse salt stands in dramatic and delicious contrast to sweet flavors such as chocolate or fruit. It works best when there's something to adhere to, as when sprinkled onto chip toppings and drizzles.

Smoked salt comes in all textures, from fine to coarse, and in a variety of wood-smoked flavors. It's easy to find, and it adds pronounced barbecue flavor to chips. Hickory and applewood smoked salts carry a distinct bacon flavor, while alderwood salt is reminiscent of smoked salmon.

CELERY SEED

Actually the seed of the lovage plant, celery seed imparts an intense celery flavor to chips. Its bright, fresh essence makes it another top ingredient in popular seasoning salts. You should always pinch celery seed between your fingers to release the essential oils. You can substitute celery salt for celery seed, but the salt will become the driver, and its flavor isn't as bright. Because celery salt is mostly salt, you'll need to reduce the other salt called for in the recipe.

GARLIC POWDER AND ONION POWDER

These guys are in almost every commercial seasoning salt. Their concentrated nature adds pleasing depth to recipes. I'm not suggesting that fresh onion and garlic shouldn't be used whenever possible, but you need dry seasonings to sprinkle over chips. Going from fresh to dry, the garlic and onion flavors deepen to rich and toasty. That's why both incarnations—fresh and dried—show up in dips, toppings, and drizzle recipes.

PAPRIKA

Smoked paprika is the key to barbecue-flavored chips. The intense smoked flavor typically comes from oak, and it's pretty concentrated stuff—a little goes a long way. Pair it with un-smoked paprika in seasoning blends to get a lot of paprika richness without obscuring other flavors with smoke.

Sweet paprika, generally referred to as regular paprika, is a mild-to-no-heat chili powder. It's a standard ingredient in commercial seasoning salts. **Hot paprika** generally delivers moderate heat, but the heat factor can vary from brand to brand depending on the pepper variety it's made from. Both hot and sweet versions can range from light and fruity to deep and peppery. Paprika adds exciting color, so look for the brightest, reddest ones available. The flavor and color of paprika bloom brightest in the presence of oil—a plus for chip seasoning.

CHILI POWDER

Chili powder is a deceptive name for what's actually a spice blend of various chili peppers plus cumin, oregano, garlic, and salt. This mixture

creates the flavor that folks associate with chili-the-stew and chili-the-hotdog topping. That's why it's a splendid chip seasoning on its own or added to spice blends such as barbecue and nacho flavorings. When a recipe calls for a single ground chili—such as ancho chili powder—don't substitute chili powder unless the other savory spices in the blend are appropriate. Old Bay Seasoning, with bay leaf and sage, is a nice alternative to chili powder.

TOMATO POWDER

This tangy topping consists of dehydrated tomatoes that have been ground into powder. It's the flavor base for nacho chips, barbecue chips, and, of course, ketchup chips. Tomato powder has spotty shelf availability. In some regions it's sold in bulk for making homemade ketchup and sauces, while in other areas it's difficult to find. Look for it in specialty food stores, spice shops, and kitchen stores. It's also available online from several inexpensive sources. If you have a dehydrator, you can totally DIY tomato powder from tomato paste.

ACIDS

If you read snack-food labels, especially chip labels, you'll likely find a variety of acids listed. This is not a bad thing. Lemon juice and vinegar provide essential tartness to beverages, dressings, and sauces, right? So how do you deliver that tartness when liquids can't be used? You use a powder. That's what gives salt-and-vinegar chips their vinegar flavor.

Citric acid comes from (guess what?) citrus fruit. It's what gives lemons their pucker power. A little goes a long way—it should be added by small measures and pinches. You can find it in the bulk-spice section of most health-food stores. It's also sold as sour salt in the kosher section of the grocery store. **Ascorbic acid** is vitamin C by another name and can be used like citric acid. It's available at most health-food stores, and grocery stores often stock it with the canning supplies. Make sure the kind you buy isn't packaged with sugar.

Acetic acid, usually sold as vinegar powder, is just that—vinegar with the water removed. It's the essential flavor in salt-and-vinegar chips. Acetic acid is not as easy to find on shelves as citric acid, but some specialty-food markets and kitchen stores carry it as vinegar powder. It's ridiculously easy to find online, and inexpensive. There, you can choose from a variety of powders, including malt vinegar, balsamic vinegar, cider vinegar, and rice vinegar.

NUTRITIONAL YEAST

Because the name is fairly off-putting, some folks call this stuff "nooch." The yeast is grown from molasses, then "killed," dried, and packaged. Nutritional yeast is a good source of protein and vitamins, including B-vitamins, and is gluten free. But that's not the point. Nooch has a rich, nutty, cheesy flavor that makes it a favorite in vegan recipes. Its satisfying savor is akin to that of miso and soy sauce, which share the same glutamic and amino acids that create the umami sensation in the mouth. When added to spice blends, nutritional yeast spikes all the flavors. It comes in flake and powder form. Powder is best for chip seasoning, but flake yeast can easily be ground between the fingers or in a food mill. You can find nutritional yeast in bulk-food bins and health-food stores. Do not substitute brewer's yeast for nutritional yeast! Brewer's yeast is alive and can cause digestive distress.

CHEESE FLAVORINGS

Who doesn't love a cheese-flavored chip? The tastes we all adore—sharp cheddar, white cheddar, and nacho cheese—are added to chips in powder form.

Cheese powders are made in a variety of ways and sold in different forms. A search online will pull up a remarkable range of flavors—cheddar, white cheddar, blue cheese—all of which can be ordered inexpensively. Finding the same variety in stores isn't as simple. Look for cheese powders or blends in bulk-spice bins, or in kitchen stores and gourmet markets. In the grocery store, try the spice aisle. You're bound to find cheese-flavored popcorn seasonings there, but be wary of them—some are essentially salt.

A brilliant hack is to lift the cheese packet from a box of macaroni-and-cheese mix. For less than a dollar—cheaper than the salty stuff in spice jars—you'll get about $1/3$ cup of cheese powder. Plus, you'll have an excuse to make homemade mac-and-cheese with the orphaned noodles.

Buttermilk powder is a common baking supply easily found in stores. It has a tangy, rich dairy flavor that's delicious on chips. It typically comes in large containers, but it keeps for a long time in the refrigerator and can be used for baking and for making soups and dressings. **Sour cream powder** has a richer, creamier flavor than buttermilk powder, but it's not as common. The two can be used interchangeably. If you have a food dehydrator, you can make your own by spreading sour cream on non-stick tray covers, drying it until it's solid, and then grinding it in a food mill.

I'm not sure why people scoff at the stuff that comes in the little green canisters—I think that grated **Parmesan** and **Romano** cheeses are both great! I call them shaker cheese. These cheeses have their own discrete usefulness because they're dry and concentrated, and pack a lot of tangy flavor. If you want to use one as a chip seasoning, simply run it through a food mill or food processor to transform it into a fine powder.

PEPPERS

Black pepper is one of the most popular condiments in the Western world, second only to salt. It's in about every recipe in this book, even some of the sweet ones. It's always best ground-on-demand. **White pepper** is hotter than black, but it has fewer flavor notes. That being said, white pepper has a funky, almost truffle-porky flavor that adds a lot to seasoning blends. **Cayenne pepper** is a chili powder that's supposed to be very hot, but its heat factor can vary a lot according to quality and age. The recipes call for sparing amounts of it, so if you're a fan of spicy-hotness, use these measurements as a starting point.

The Top 5 Flavors

Here are the classics—the top five chip flavor blends. These are the granddaddies in the snack pantheon. In fact, Sour Cream & Onion, Barbecue, and Salt & Vinegar were the very first chip flavors, introduced in the 1950s. Before then, there was only Salt. Soon after came Ranch and Nacho Cheese flavors in the 1960s.

BARBECUE
MAKES ABOUT 4 TABLESPOONS

- 2 teaspoons smoked paprika
- 2 teaspoons sweet or hot paprika, to taste
- 2 teaspoons Old Bay® Seasoning (substitute chili powder)
- 2 teaspoons brown sugar
- 1 teaspoon mustard powder
- 1 teaspoon nutritional yeast
- 1/2 teaspoon freshly ground black pepper
- 1/2 teaspoon onion powder
- 1/2 teaspoon table salt or fine sea salt
- 1/4 teaspoon ascorbic acid, citric acid, or acetic acid (vinegar powder)
- 1/4 teaspoon garlic powder
- 1/8 teaspoon turmeric

☐ Mix the ingredients together, and then store the topping in an airtight container. For finer powder that really sticks to chips, grind the ingredients in a food mill for 2 or 3 seconds.

SOUR CREAM & ONION
MAKES ABOUT 4 TABLESPOONS

- 2 tablespoons buttermilk or sour cream powder
- 2 teaspoons dried chives (preferably freeze dried)
- 1 teaspoon Parmesan and Romano cheese (the boxed kind)
- 1 teaspoon onion powder
- 1 teaspoon dehydrated onion flakes
- 1 teaspoon table salt or fine sea salt
- 1 teaspoon nutritional yeast, optional
- 1/8 teaspoon ascorbic acid, citric acid, or acetic acid (vinegar powder)

☐ Mix the ingredients together, and then store the topping in an airtight container. For a finer powder, grind the ingredients in a food mill for 1 or 2 seconds.

RANCH
☐ Follow the Sour Cream & Onion recipe and add:

- 1 teaspoon parsley flakes
- 1/4 teaspoon garlic powder
- 1/4 teaspoon celery seed
- 1/4 teaspoon black pepper

SALT & VINEGAR
MAKES ABOUT 2 TABLESPOONS

- 1 tablespoon kosher salt
- 2 teaspoons chunky sea salt
- 1 teaspoon nutritional yeast
- 1 teaspoon ascorbic acid, citric acid, or acetic acid (vinegar powder)
- 1/2 teaspoon sugar

☐ Combine the ingredients in a sturdy zip-top bag and then crush some of the larger chunks of salt with a rolling pin. You can also grind the ingredients in a food mill for 2 or 3 seconds, leaving some larger specks of salt.

NACHO CHEESE
MAKES ABOUT 4 TABLESPOONS

- 2 tablespoons nutritional yeast
- 1 tablespoon Parmesan and Romano cheese (the boxed kind)
- 2 teaspoons buttermilk powder, sour cream powder, or cheese powder (see Cheese Flavorings, page 23)
- 2 teaspoons chili powder
- 1 teaspoon sweet or hot paprika (bright red is best)
- 1 teaspoon table salt or fine sea salt
- 1 teaspoon brown sugar
- 1/2 teaspoon ground cumin
- 1/2 teaspoon garlic powder
- 1/2 teaspoon dry mustard
- 1/2 teaspoon onion powder
- 1/8 teaspoon ascorbic or citric acid
- 1/8 teaspoon cayenne powder, or to taste

☐ Mix the ingredients together, and then store the topping in an airtight container. For a finer powder, grind the ingredients in a food mill for 2 or 3 seconds.

GENERAL CHIP MAKING TECHNIQUES

CUTTING

The key to successful chips is in the cutting. Cut them too thick, and you could end up with tough or rubbery chips that won't be done in the recipe's specified time. Cut them too thin, and they may burn before the time's up. That said, erring on the side of too thin is better than going thick. Whatever thickness you choose, stick with it. Don't vary it within a batch, or some of your chips will burn before others are done. Most importantly, cut your slices evenly, with no thick or thin parts.

So that's the challenge. If you already have good knife skills, you're in fine shape. Otherwise, I suggest that you gather more than the recipe specifies of whatever you're chipping and then practice, practice, practice. Most of the chips in this book can be cut with a wide, sharp knife and a steady hand. If all goes well, you'll have extra chips; if not, you can cull out the duds.

CHIP TIP: The food you're slicing needs to sit still and be stable so that you can make steady, even cuts. Create a flat base for it by slicing a thin sliver, about 1/4 inch, from one side. Then position the food on this base and commence cutting.

If knife skills aren't your strong suit, get some backup. A mandoline is a chipper's best friend and having one makes the process a breeze. You'll probably get tired of my prodding in the recipes about using a mandoline, but it really does a remarkable job. Even if you have the moves of a master sushi chef, you're likely to reach for your mandoline because of its effortless perfection—and because it's fun to use.

A food processor equipped with a thin-cutting disk can make chipping fast and precise. Read more about food processors in Key Tools on page 10.

A sharp and sturdy vegetable peeler is also handy for chip cutting. To slice chips, trim the produce to match the blade width, if necessary, and make a flat base on one side. Put the produce on your working surface and hold it steady between your fingers. Pull the peeler toward you, bearing down and making even swipes across the surface. When the cutter can't go any deeper, raise the produce you're cutting up on a pedestal—a flat knife handle makes a perfect perch.

SOAKING

Starchy vegetables should be soaked in water to remove the surface starch that's released during cutting and to extract the soluble starch and sugars near the surface. Potatoes, taro, and yucca are high-starch foods that require soaking. (For information about starch-wrangling in potatoes, see page 40.) Fruits and vegetables that darken or brown when cut also need to be soaked, either in water to prevent air contact, as with potatoes, or in acidified water to prevent browning, as with apples.

Measuring up with Metrics

The ideal thin chip for these recipes is about $1/16$ inch thick. Heftier chips are about $1/8$ inch thick. A simple way to demonstrate these thicknesses is with a quarter (the coin), but in order to demonstrate I need to switch to metrics because that's how coins and many kitchen cutters are measured.

A U.S. quarter is 1.75 mm thick.
> **(A Canadian quarter is 1.6 mm thick.)**

$1/16$ inch rounds up 1.6 mm, about the
> **thickness of a quarter.**

$1/8$ inch rounds up to 3.2 mm, about the
> **thickness of 2 stacked quarters.**

Many food-processor blades are measured in metrics, with 2 mm being the thinnest cutting thickness for most models. The next size up is 4 mm, which is really too thick for most chips. European and Asian mandoline cutting blade settings are metric as well—some start as thin as .75 mm. For models with free-moving blades and no thickness settings, use a ruler or the quarter trick as guides for setting the blade distance.

DRYING

For fried chip recipes, it's extremely important that only dry slices go into oil—wet slices will bubble out of control when they make contact. For baked chip recipes, the slices usually need to be dried before they can be seasoned and cooked. A salad spinner does a good job of pre-drying, but the only way to remove all the water is with kitchen towels or sturdy paper towels (if you don't mind the waste). Spread the slices out on the towel and blot them with another towel.

SEASONING

The critical moment for adding salt or seasonings to chips is while they're in an expansive stage—when they've just come out of the oven or fryer and are still glistening. For those few seconds, the surface moisture and oil get a chance to mingle with the seasoning. Then the cooling chip draws the seasoning tighter to its surface. If you wait to season after the chips are cool, more of the precious morsels will fall off.

STORING

Most chips can be stored for days or weeks after cooking—that is, if you're a person of great self-control. Allow the chips to cool and dry out at room temperature for 30 minutes to an hour and then store them in airtight containers. Chips that tend to get sticky, such as strawberry, star fruit, or pear chips, should be stored between waxed paper or parchment layers.

REJUVENATING

While most chips hold their crisp edge for a decent amount of time, some go limp soon after they're cooked because all of the moisture wasn't cooked out, or because they've been exposed to humidity. You can recapture that freshly made flavor and crunch by spreading the chips out on a rimmed baking sheet in a single layer and heating them for 5 to 7 minutes in a 350°F oven. This is also a great way to liven up store-bought chips—especially tortilla chips.

Scalding for Lighter Chips

Snack enthusiasts and food-science geeks spend a lot of time pondering ways to make a better potato chip. For many of us, the Holy Grail is a homemade version of the perfect, barely golden chip we love to eat by the bagful. Achieving that kind of delectable perfection involves factors like starch and sugar control, and whether or not the potatoes used are high in amylose. (Amy who? See A Tale of Two Starches on page 40.)

Soaking slices in cool or warm water rinses off the starch and sugars that get released when the potato cells are sliced open. Soaking is a good way to prevent dark chips. But to get buttery, golden chips, still more starch has to go; for this, you need hot water, which will pull starch from the uncut cells near the potato's surface. You also need to use all-purpose potatoes that are less waxy, such as Kennebec and All Blue, or floury potatoes, like russets, that are high in water-soluble amylose.

Par-boiling your potato slices is an effective way of getting rid of extra starch. Virtually all of the starch comes out, and the chips fry up to a pale tawny gold. But par-boiling also extracts flavor from the chips and hurts their texture. At temperatures above 180°F, starch cells rupture, dissolve, and lose their ability to draw in oil, which is the secret to delectable chips. The busted cells also send spud flavors into the water. Another drawback to this method is that paper-thin slices of potato can easily become crumbly or dissolve altogether while boiling.

Luckily, there's another way: scalding. With this method, you're going for a magic temperature of around 150° to 160°F (just a bit warmer than hot tap water, which is 120° to 130°F), which will activate starch release without busting cells. The time it takes to expel the starch is short—only 2 to 3 minutes. Sufficiently scalded slices then go into cold tap water, and the process is complete. This method is simple and fairly forgiving, but you have to stay within the limits: keep the wwater under 180°F, scald no longer than 5 minutes, and you're golden.

SCALDING METHOD

☐ Prepare and slice the potatoes (or starchy vegetable) and submerge them in water.

☐ Heat a large pot of water (3 to 4 quarts) over medium heat. Add ¼ cup distilled vinegar. Have a cooking thermometer handy, preferably attached to the pot. Bring the water temperature to between 160°F and 170°F degrees. This won't take long if you start with hot tap water.

☐ Add ¼ cup distilled vinegar to the water.

☐ While the water heats, drain the potato slices in a colander and rinse them under hot running water. This preheats them so that they won't lower the scalding-water bath temperature.

☐ Fill a large bowl or pot with cold water.

☐ When the pot of scalding water is ready, drop in the potato slices and turn off the heat. (Move the pot off the burner if you're not cooking with gas.) Wait 2 to 3 minutes.

☐ Drain the slices through a colander and transfer them to the cold water. Let the slices sit for 2 to 3 minutes.

That's it. You can dry and fry the slices, or let them sit in the water until you're ready to use them.

BAKING

BAKING SPEED

Some chips can be turned out quickly in a hot oven, while others take more time and attention. **Hot & fast** works fine for some of the recipes, and rates high on the instant-gratification scale. The temperature ranges from 400°F to 300°F. Depending on the food and its thickness, baked chips generally take less than 30 minutes per batch. **Low & slow** is the way to go for high-moisture and high-sugar foods, such as apples, star fruit, and pears. This process provides longer exposure to heat, allowing water to dissipate before sugars begin to brown. The low & slow temperature range tops out at around 275°F and goes down to 200F° (or as low as your oven will go). Slow-cooking at lower temperatures is a good plan for any chip. It's the best way to ensure that the food dries out enough to become crisp before the sugars over-brown or burn.

ADJUSTING FOR FACTORS

The success of these recipes depends on some variables—how dry or moist the slices are, how much or little sugar and starch they have, and most importantly, how thick or thin you've sliced the chips. If you cut them thicker than the recipe suggests, you'll need to allow more time for them to bake. If your chips are browning too quickly, turn down the oven a bit and perhaps rotate the pans more often. The slower they bake, the more control you have over the finished product. So it's okay, even ideal, to slow down a hot-&-fast recipe by decreasing the temperature and giving the chips more time. But you should never speed up a low-&-slow recipe.

OVEN EVENNESS

Most ovens don't cook evenly, and nothing demonstrates this quality better than baking paper-thin pieces of food inside one. Typically, the back of an oven is hotter than the front, and the top is hotter than the bottom. The fact that, for most of the recipes in this book, two baking pans are in play and affecting airflow can add to an oven's inconsistency. Here's how to average out the highs and lows. Start by placing the baking pans in the upper and lower thirds of the oven, each positioned away from the center and toward (but not touching) the oven walls. While you bake, switch everything up—turn the pans back-to-front and move them to opposite racks. The recipes cue you when to do this, but you may decide to do it more often. If you have a magic oven, you might not need to move the pans at all.

Minuses and Pluses of Baked Chips

Full disclosure. Baked chips can be tricky. Moisture content and chip thickness affect their cooking time, which can be considerably less or more than the recipe states. With every batch of baked chips, you can take it for granted that some will come out with soft-ish centers, and some will have browner-than-ideal edges. Also, the chips generally shrink a lot. Now that you know the obstacles involved, here's the upside: The seasonings you add get baked into each chip. Another plus: Baked chips deliver that distinctively delicious roasted flavor.

BAKED CHIPS STEP-BY-STEP

1. Cut thin, even slices.

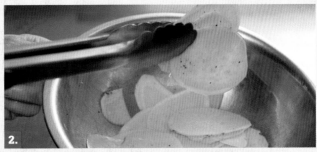

2. For sturdy slices, toss them with oil and seasonings.

3. Line baking sheets with silcone baking mats or parchment paper.

4. Arrange the slices in a single layer.

5. For delicate slices, brush them with oil and sprinkle on seasonings.

6. Offset the baking sheets, place in upper and lower thirds of oven.

FRYING

OIL DEPTH

An ideal depth for oil in a Dutch oven or fryer is about 1¹/₂ to 2 inches. There's rarely a need for more oil than that, and you can certainly fry with less. But a more generous amount of oil helps maintain even heat and ensures less of a drop in temperature when new food is added. For shallower pans, such as skillets, oil depth needs to be ³/₄ to 1 inch in order to keep at least 1 inch of headspace above the oil. For an average-size wok, 1¹/₂ to 2 inches of oil at the deepest point provides plenty of surface area for frying and a nice well of oil to maintain even heat.

THERMOMETER

There are ways to judge the frying temperature without a thermometer, but when cooking with hot oil, why not be sure? You'll feel more in control of the process when you know the numbers: the precise moment when the oil is ready for a batch of chips, exactly how much the oil temperature drops when food goes in, and when the temperature has recovered. And for safety's sake, you should know your oil's smoke point—the hazardous line where oil breaks down and turns bad.

Clip the thermometer to the side of the pot, preferably on the back side and out of the way of the cooking action.

HEATING THE OIL

The length of time it takes to reach frying temperature depends on the volume of oil and the thickness of your vessel. I like to bring the temperature up slowly over low or medium-low heat to about 200°F and then hold it there while I prepare other parts of the recipe and set up my cooking area. Once everything's set for frying, I turn up the heat to medium-high to quickly reach the recipe's frying temperature. This method calls for keeping tabs on the oil temperature for an extended time, which may not suit you. You should avoid bringing the oil to frying temperature before all the ingredients are prepared and everything is in place for frying. This prolongs the time that the oil is exposed to high temperatures.

Headspace

On contact with hot oil, the water inside food immediately turns to steam, which, as it rises to the top, creates a layer of bubbles. The side of your cooking vessel needs to be high enough to contain the bubbles—that safety zone is the headspace. A rule of thumb is that the headspace should be more than double the oil depth, and more is better. For a Dutch oven, that's about 3 inches above the oil, and for a wok, that's at least 3 inches of rim around the oil. Some recipes will call for more headspace.

CROWDING

In most cases, you want to put only about a single layer of raw slices in the oil at once. This prevents the temperature from dropping too much and makes it easier to keep the slices from sticking together. Smaller batches are easier to keep up with as they cook and faster coming out of the oil once they're done—there's less chance of overcooking.

TEMPERATURE DROP

When a batch of raw slices enters the oil, the temperature immediately drops. The time it takes the oil to return to frying temperature is known as the recovery time. Chips are thin, so recovery is usually short, but if too may raw slices go into the oil at once, they can get oil-logged, stick together, or break if recovery is too slow. To make everything come together without a hitch, turn your burner to high just before you drop in the slices, and be sure the oil has pegged the frying temperature and is heading up. Interestingly, the second batch usually doesn't drop the temperature as much as the first, likely because the frying vessel itself has become warmer.

TURNING

Chips need to stay on the move. For most of the recipes in this book, you'll be told to constantly move and turn the chips. Slices sometimes stick together for the first few seconds they're in the oil because the surface sugars and starches are melting together. So keep them separated. You might notice that with potatoes and other starchy foods that chips hit a brief, fragile stage when they're easily broken. If this happens, handle them gently for a few seconds until they harden a little.

FRYING PROCESS

Chip slices should bubble rapidly on contact with oil—if they don't, the oil isn't hot enough. At first, the water inside the slices turns to steam, which creates a lot of noisy, steamy bubbles. As the water cooks out, the bubbling slows and eventually stops. When things calm down, the chips crisp up and take on color. At this point, things really happen quickly—chips can go from golden to overcooked in a few seconds. So, as the bubbling subsides, be ready to transfer the chips to the draining surface.

DRAINING

Fried chips need to drain briefly after they come out of the oil. Just a minute or two on absorbent paper is enough to draw out excess oil. (Draining may also wick away some of the fried-food guilt, if you're susceptible to that.) One of the first instructions you'll find in the fried-chip recipes is to set up a draining station near your cooktop. Proximity is important here. The motion from pot to draining station needs to be short and direct because some oil will invariably drip from the chips along the way. Positioning the station next to the oil is ideal but not always possible. Just think it through and set up the clearest path possible.

Assemble the draining station on a baking sheet or sturdy tray. This will give you the ability to move it around if necessary. Line the baking sheet or tray with paper towels, paper bags, or newspapers. I like to use a paper bag topped with a paper towel, which I replace when it gets soggy. On top of the paper you should place a wire cooling rack, turned upside down. With this setup, the wire grid will push down on the paper, creating a flat surface so the chips can't congregate over pockets of oil.

FRYING STEP-BY-STEP

1. Cut thin, even slices.

2. Soak starchy foods in water.

6. When the oil is ready, add the slices.

7. Constantly stir and turn the chips while they fry.

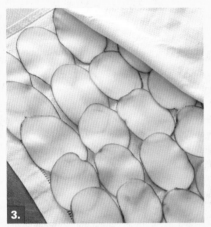

3. Arrange the slices on a kitchen towel.

4. Roll and blot them until they're dry.

5. Prepare a drain station for frying.

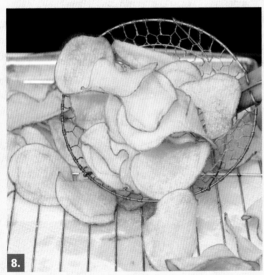

8. Transfer the chips to the draining station.

9. Season the chips the second they come out of the oil.

Cool-Start Frying

Here's an all-in-one approach to forcing water and sugars out of potatoes and other starchy vegetables using gentle heat: Put your slices into 200°F oil and take them out when they reach about 350°F. Starting out under the boiling point gives the potato slices a chance to gently poach. As they get warmer, the water and sugars are drawn from cells near the surface. The oil goes into those empty cells, making the chips crispy. With much of the sugar taken away, the chips are more likely to come out golden brown.

As frying goes, this is a pretty laid-back method. Everything starts out nice and slow, with none of that quick, sizzling-on-contact action. It's pretty uncomplicated too. The heat rises gradually, the chips start to sizzle, then fry, and then they're done. You can cook a few more chips per batch this way because you don't have to factor in how raw ingredients may lower the oil temperature. Also, the oil is more gently treated, spending very little time edging near temperatures that break down quality.

METHOD

❑ Slice, soak, and dry the potato slices, and set up a draining station as described in Classic Chips (see page 43).

❑ Add about two inches of oil to a wide, heavy pot, leaving at least 2 inches of headspace above the oil. Clip on a cooking thermometer and bring the temperature up to 200°F over medium-low heat.

❑ Drop about 2 layers of slices into the oil—they should sink to the bottom. Turn the heat to medium-high and move the slices around with a slotted spoon or spider until slow bubbles start to rise from the potatoes. At this point, you should avoid touching them until they show color and begin to fry.

CHIP TIP: The potatoes start out poaching when the oil rises above the boiling point (212°F). Like boiled potatoes, they soften and become breakable. At about 250°F, they begin to firm up, and you can resume moving and turning them in the oil.

❑ As the chips fry, they'll bubble rapidly, curl up, and rise to the top. Keep them moving. When the oil gets to around 325°F to 350°F, the bubbling will slow, and the chips will turn a light golden brown. They're done. Turn the heat back to low and immediately transfer the chips to the draining surface. Sprinkle them with salt and seasonings.

❑ Prepare for the next batch. Allow the oil to return to 200°F. If there's a lot of residue at the bottom of the pot, remove it. Then make space for more chips on your draining surface.

❑ The chips will get crisper as they cool, so wait a few minutes before serving. Allow them to cool completely before you store them in an airtight container. They'll keep for a couple of weeks.

DEHYDRATING

There are two excellent reasons for making chips in a food dehydrator: They come out looking fresh and vibrant, and it's nearly impossible burn them. Also, the margin of error is measured in hours rather than seconds.

LOADING THE OVEN

In most cases, the slices can be placed on trays so that they overlap slightly because they will shrink considerably. The trays in stacked-tray models need to be rearranged at least once during the process—move the bottom trays to the top. Most box-style models with drawer trays don't need to be rearranged, but check your instructions.

COOKING TIMES

It's impossible to offer firm cooking times for dehydrated chip recipes—there are too many variables. Brands and models perform differently according to their design. External factors such as room temperature and humidity also affect cooking time. Factoring in the variables, the same recipe could take one chip-maker six hours and another 24 or more.

OIL AND SEASONINGS

Regardless of the claims that good chips can be made in a dehydrator without oil, the truth is that what comes out is nothing more than dehydrated vegetables. Better chips are made with a bit of oil—not a lot. Oil adds savory flavor and distributes the seasonings, and it makes the chips pleasingly crunchy rather than just brittle. Unlike baked or fried, dehydrated chips should be seasoned before they cook, rather than after.

Dehydrator as Seasoning Factory

An added benefit of owning a food dehydrator is that you can use it to make chip seasonings. Herbs are an obvious choice, but other flavorful foods such as scallions, tomatoes, or horseradish dry marvelously and come out ready to be powdered and sprinkled over chips. Cheese can be dried on paper towels (make sure you change the towels once or twice as they fill with oil) and then pulverized into cheese powder. Also— almost like magic—you can dry creamy things, including ketchup, steak sauce, sriracha chili sauce, or sour cream, on non-stick tray covers and then grind them into flavor powders. Check out the recipe for Bloody Mary Powder (page 80).

DEHYDRATING STEP-BY-STEP

1.
Cut thin, even slices.

2.
Arrange the slices close on the drying trays and spray or brush them with oil.

3.
Add seasonings and place the trays in the dehydrator.

RECIPES

Recipe chapters fill the rest of the book, the first one dedicated to nothing but the Mighty POTATO. You'll find a fully loaded primer-style chapter on all things potato—which ones to use, how to buy and store them, and how to prepare them for chipping. The recipes cover all the chip-making techniques and their variations.

In VEGGIES you'll learn the secret of lotus roots (hint: not a root) and the best chip-making mushrooms. There's a chapter-within-a-chapter on making chips from leafy greens with info on the best greens to use.

The FRUIT chapter includes some sweet delights. A bonus with fruit chips is their pair-up potential with other desserts. All it takes is a jewel-like star fruit chip, a trio of technicolor strawberry chips,

or a hand-toss of spicy toasted coconut chips to turn a nice enough cupcake or pretty good bowl of ice cream into an out-of-this-world dessert.

MEAT & CHEESE introduces some unusual twists like discovering how to combine cheese with tasty morsels (capers, green peppercorns, black walnuts) to make amazing chips and how to take sausages and meats to the next level.

Last chapter, READYMADE, is a collection of recipes that start with grab-and-go prepared foods—wonton wrappers, tortillas, bagels, and pitas.

Use these recipes in a mix-and-match style. Switch out the cooking methods. Recast the seasonings from one recipe to another. Alter the dip recipes to make them your own.

OH, MIGHTY POTATO!

Plentiful, versatile, and familiar, the potato has long been a supper-table standby—a can't-fail comfort food that has always clicked with consumers. The details surrounding its rise to snack-chip stardom are open to speculation (see Potato Chip History, page 58). Although no one knows for sure who sliced and fried the first potato chip, the process created a classic—one of the first industrially manufactured, nationally distributed snack foods.

As the premier snack of the modern age, the potato chip is regularly analyzed in laboratories and taste tests. Every aspect of a chip is evaluated, including thickness, texture, salt-to-fat ratio, quality of crunch, and the ways in which a chip's shape and size relate to a taster's tongue. These are important factors to consider when it comes to making potato chips, and—as you'll see in the pages that follow—I try to be mindful of them as I fry and bake my own. Some of the recipes contain science-based techniques, but they're not the kind you have to track with a spreadsheet.

In the land of chips, potatoes rule. That's why they're the starting point for this culinary journey. As versatile vehicles of flavor, they're compatible with the many spice blends, toppings, drizzles, and dips you'll find recipes for in this book. They're also easy to obtain, easy to cut, and easy to cook. What's not to love about the mighty spud? Let's make some chips!

THE POTATO KINGDOM

Most supermarkets offer an exciting selection of potatoes, including heirloom varieties from around the world. Make sure you buy the freshest ones you can find—once potatoes come out of the ground, their starch starts turning to sugar. Buying them fresh from a farmers' market is ideal. You should avoid potatoes that have been refrigerated (see Potato Storage on page 40).

Floury potatoes, also categorized as starchy or mealy potatoes, have the lowest water content and high levels of amylose starch, which makes the starch granules inside heat-sensitive and quick to release their water and sugars. This type of potato is excellent for fried and high-temperature baked chips. Russet (sometimes called Idaho) potatoes rule the entire category here. Beware of old-in-the-tooth russets, or ones that have been stored in the fridge.

Waxy potatoes contain the most water and highest amount of amylopectin, which makes their starch granules tough and heat tolerant. When cooked, waxy potatoes hold onto water and remain firm. This makes them poor candidates for fried chips and chips baked at high temperatures because the sugars and starch in the potato will burn before the water is cooked out and the chips get crisp. Waxy potatoes should be cooked at a low temperature to provide time for the moisture to evaporate and the chips to turn crispy. Waxy varieties include Red Bliss, Fingerlings, and Finns.

All-purpose potatoes are the in-betweeners. Varieties in this group span the gap between starchy and waxy. Some are better for frying, while others work as slow-baked chips. The potatoes should be fresh. Good varieties for fried chips include All Blue and Kennebec. Yukon Gold and Purple Peruvian are good for both frying and high-temperature baking.

Like floury potatoes, **sweet potatoes** have a very high amylose content. They give up their moisture easily, making them excellent chippers. But they also contain more sugar and tend to brown quickly, so be sure to soak and rinse them well. If you're frying them, consider scalding them in hot water first to remove as much sugar as possible (see page 27). Good varieties are the Jewel, Stokes Purple, which is purple throughout, and the yellowish, dry Hannah, which isn't as sweet as other sweet potatoes.

A Tale of Two Starches

All potatoes contain some sugar and a lot of starch, which is a complex form of sugar. The starch in potatoes comes in two structures—as amylose or amylopectin. (I know this sounds complicated, but stay with me.) Amylose is assembled in simple chains of molecules that easily break when exposed to heat and water. When a potato with a high amylose content is exposed to hot water, or to high heat, its starch granules break apart and release its water and sugars. Floury potatoes, such as Russets, contain mostly amylose.

The starch in waxy potatoes is almost entirely amylopectin, which is bound together in complicated knots of molecules that insulate its starch granules when they're exposed to water and heat. The tough granules stay together in hot water, and the sugars and moisture are held securely within. Likewise, in a hot oven or fryer, amylopectin's tough structure delays dehydration and keeps the water and sugars inside. If cooked too quickly, the waterlogged sugars will burn, which can result in soggy chips.

POTATO STORAGE

Potatoes should be kept in a cool, dry place, ideally at a temperature between 45° and 60°F. They should be allowed to get air but not light. Putting them in a brown paper bag and stashing them in a dark corner is a good plan. Use them within a couple of weeks. You should never use refrigerated potatoes for chips! When potatoes are stored at a temperature below 40°F, their starch converts to sugar, which makes them darken quickly when cooked. If they're refrigerated for too long, the sugar will spread throughout their interiors, creating permanent dark rings that instantly cook to cocoa brown. Don't risk it! Use fresh potatoes.

TO PEEL OR NOT

The skin of a potato cooks darker and imparts a browner, toastier flavor that you may like in your chips. Just know that conventionally grown potatoes can be exposed to pesticides and fungicides from the farm to the packing plant. Unless you know where your potatoes are grown or you buy organic, peeling is a good idea.

CHIP THICKNESS

Those stout kettle-style chips you get at the grocery store are about 1/8 inch thick and have a deeper, browner flavor because they're cooked longer. If thick is your thing, use really fresh Russets and rinse them well. Consider using the scalding method (See Scalding for Lighter Chips, page 27) to remove extra starch or the slow-fry method (see Cool-Start Frying, page 34) to crisp them slowly. This is also a good thickness for baked potato chips cooked at lower temperatures—325°F or lower.

Thin potato chips are especially delectable and have an exhilarating crunch. But if you cut your potatoes too thin, the resulting chips may be too delicate, especially if you're dipping or adding drizzles or toppings. About 1/16 inch is a good thickness. Thin chips cook very quickly, making it all the more important for the slices to be cut evenly.

SOAKING AND RINSING

Water is important to potato-chip-making. It prevents peeled potatoes from turning dark and removes the starch and sugars that are released from a potato's cells during cutting. Exposing the slices to hot water and acid accelerates starch release.

As you cut chips, keep the potato slices submerged in hot water to prevent browning and to begin drawing out the starch. When you're finished with cutting, drain and rinse the slices, then cover them again with hot water—the hottest water that comes from your tap. Add distilled vinegar and soak the slices for 15 to 20 minutes (you can hold them in the water until you're ready to cook them). As the potatoes soak you'll actually see the milky starch settling in the bottom of the bowl. Drain the slices, rinse them under the hottest water you can stand, and dry them.

Alternately, you can opt for a more extreme soaking treatment that removes even more starch by scalding the slices in heated water on the stove (see Scalding for Lighter Chips, page 27).

WHAT TURNS CHIPS BROWN?

As sugar cooks, it caramelizes—a transformative process during which it goes from golden to golden brown, then to bitterly brown, and finally to carbon black. Because potatoes contain a lot of starch— a form of sugar—they can jump to the bitter stage before all of the moisture has been cooked out. This is particularly true for chips that are fried or baked at high temperatures. So it's important to use drier potatoes and to soak them well.

DRYING

When you're ready to dry your slices, spread them evenly on a kitchen towel and blot them with another towel. Roll them up and press down gently to blot some more. For frying recipes, to prevent the slices from darkening and to draw out more starch, you can hold the slices in the towel until you are ready to cook them. Unroll them just before frying—your slices will be nicely separated and ready to drop into the oil.

1.

Potato starch will settle to the bottom.

2.

Drain and rinse the potatoes until no starch remains.

3.

Unsoaked starchy potatoes after being exposed to air for 15 minutes!

CLASSIC CHIPS WITH FIVE SHADES OF ONION DIP

PREP TIME: 5 MINUTES | SOAKING TIME: 15 MINUTES | COOKING TIME: 15 MINUTES | MAKES 8–10 CUPS

Basic and beautiful, crisp and golden—potato chips are like magic to make. Slices of raw potato, with their unappetizing starchiness, go into the pot for an exciting moment of transformation, emerging as translucent golden morsels redolent with potato chip deliciousness. Each batch is an exciting experience, and the process is almost as addictive as the treats produced. I'm waxing poetically, I know, but after making many batches of homemade potato chips, I'm here to say that store-bought chips just can't compare.

Throughout this book, you'll find many different seasoning blends that will perfectly accent your chips. You can also head directly to page 24 and pick one of the Top 5 Flavors—Barbecue, Sour Cream & Onion, Ranch, Salt & Vinegar, or Nacho Cheese.

INGREDIENTS

      Hot water for soaking
  2 tablespoons distilled vinegar
1½ pounds Russet potatoes, scrubbed
      clean or peeled
      Oil for frying
      Kosher salt or sea salt

METHOD

PREPARE THE SLICES

☐ Fill a medium-sized mixing bowl with about 2 quarts of hot tap water. Cut the potatoes into thin, even slices—1/16 inch (a quarter's thickness) is ideal for thin chips, while 1/8 inch (two quarters) is good for thicker ones. A mandoline or food processor will make this task much easier. As you cut, drop the slices into the water to prevent darkening.

CHIP TIP: **If you like, you can try the scalding technique (see Scalding for Lighter Chips, page 27) here to remove more sugars and make the lightest-colored chips possible.**

☐ Drain and replace the water with more hot water and add the vinegar. Let the slices soak for at least 15 minutes.

☐ Drain the slices into a colander and rinse them under hot water until the water runs clear of starch. Spread the potato slices across a kitchen towel and pat them dry with another towel. Roll up the slices in the towel and gently press to blot.

FRY THE CHIPS

☐ Prepare a draining surface near your cooktop by lining a baking sheet with paper towels or a paper bag. Then place a wire cooling rack on top, laid upside down. Have your salt and seasonings nearby.

☐ Pour about 1 to 1½ inches of oil into a wide, heavy pot or wok. There should be about 3 inches of headspace above the oil or 3 inches of clear rim around the wok. Attach a thermometer to the pot. Over high heat, bring the oil temperature to 360°F.

☐ Unroll the potato slices and carefully drop them into the oil. They should immediately begin bubbling. Don't crowd the pot—add just enough slices for a single layer. With a slotted spoon or spider, constantly move and turn the chips while they cook. In 2 or 3 minutes they'll begin to brown and the bubbling will begin to slow or stop. When the slices are golden brown, transfer them to the blotting surface and immediately sprinkle them with salt and seasoning.

☐ Continue frying the remaining slices, allowing the oil to return to 360°F and making room on the blotting surface for the next batch of chips. Don't forget to add seasonings to the chips as they come out of the oil.

☐ The chips will get crisper as they cool, so wait a couple of minutes before you serve them. Allow the chips to cool completely before storing them in an airtight container. They'll keep for a couple of weeks, but only if you keep them out of sight!

☐ If the chips get soft or you want to recreate that just-made experience, re-heat them in a 300°F oven for 4 or 5 minutes.

FIVE SHADES OF ONION DIP

PREP TIME: 45 MINUTES | REST TIME: 2 HOURS

MAKES ABOUT 2 CUPS

A spectrum of onion flavors is wrapped inside this dip—caramelized, fresh, dried, scallion, and bright-green chive. An unusual layer of preparation is involved in its making—carmelizing the onions—but it's a simple task that will make your kitchen smell amazing. However, if you need to feed your onion-dip jones, like, right now, take one package of onion soup mix, combine it with one pint of sour cream, and dive in! It's the golden formula for a classic flavor. But if you're in the mood to make something truly remarkable, I give you Five Shades of Onion Dip.

INGREDIENTS

- 3 tablespoons butter
- 2^1/$_2$ cups (2 medium) finely diced yellow or sweet onion
- ^{1}/$_2$ teaspoon freshly ground black pepper
- ^{1}/$_4$ teaspoon ground white pepper
- 1 tablespoon balsamic vinegar
- 1 tablespoon Worcestershire sauce
- ^{3}/$_4$ cup mayonnaise
- ^{3}/$_4$ cup sour cream
- ^{1}/$_4$ cup (2 ounces) cream cheese, softened
- 2 tablespoons finely chopped scallions, whites and greens
- 1 tablespoon freshly squeezed lemon juice
- 2 teaspoons finely chopped chives
- 2 teaspoons dried onion flakes
- 1 teaspoon grated onion
- ^{1}/$_2$ teaspoon kosher salt
- ^{1}/$_4$ teaspoon freshly grated or pressed garlic (substitute ^{1}/$_8$ teaspoon garlic powder)

METHOD

☐ To caramelize the onions, melt the butter in a wide skillet or sauté pan over medium-high heat. Add the onion and the black and white peppers and sauté, stirring often, until the onions begin to color—for about 5 minutes. Turn the heat to medium-low and continue cooking for another 15 minutes until the onions are soft and have a rich honey color. Every couple of minutes stir, scrape, and flatten the onions. Stir in the

balsamic vinegar and Worcestershire sauce and immediately remove the pan from the heat. Transfer the caramelized onions to a plate and let the mixture cool in the refrigerator for 5 minutes.

☐ Make the dip. In a mixing bowl, combine the caramelized onions, mayonnaise, sour cream, cream cheese, scallions, lemon juice, chives, onion flakes, grated onion, salt, and garlic. Mix to combine (a hand-held mixer or pastry blender would be helpful here), and scoop the dip into to a serving bowl.

☐ Refrigerate the dip for at least 2 hours (8 hours or overnight would be ideal) before serving to allow the flavors to meld. Let the dip warm slightly before serving. If it's too thick, stir in a teaspoon or so of liquid—milk, buttermilk, water—until it suits you. The dip will keep in the refrigerator for about a week.

What a Dip!

French Onion Dip has reigned over the chip bowl since 1952, the year Lipton gave us dehydrated onion soup mix and a California cook stirred it into a carton of sour cream. It was called California dip then (some still call it that), and the recipe spread like wildfire. I'm not sure when it became French. Anyone?

GUEST CONTRIBUTOR

Marissa Lippert (nourishkitchentable.com)

FRIED

BLUE CHIPS WITH WILD SALMON TARTAR, TRUFFLE OIL, CHIVES, AND CRÈME FRAÎCHE

PREP TIME: 15 MINUTES | FRYING TIME: 15 MINUTES | ASSEMBLY TIME: 5 MINUTES | MAKES 16–20 PIECES

INGREDIENTS

2 medium blue or purple potatoes, such as All Blue
Neutral-flavored oil for frying
Sea salt
6 ounces wild salmon, sushi grade, finely diced
1 1/2 teaspoon truffle oil
1/4 cup crème fraiche
Chives, cut into 1 1/2-inch pieces
Lemon zest
Kosher salt and freshly ground pepper to taste

METHOD

☐ Peel the potatoes, or leave them unpeeled if you prefer. Using a mandoline, cut the potatoes into slices that are about 1/8 inch thick. Drop the slices into a bowl of water as you cut and allow them to soak for a few minutes.

☐ Drain the slices and rinse them under running water for a few seconds. Then spread them out on a kitchen towel and blot them dry.

☐ Prepare a draining station near your cooktop by covering a baking sheet with absorbent paper. Lay a wire cooling rack on top, turned upside down.

☐ Pour 1/2 to 1 inch of oil into a large, heavy skillet and bring it up to about 350°F over high heat. Fry the slices in 2 to 3 batches, for about 1 to 2 minutes per batch (thinner slices may take less time). Move and turn the chips while they cook.

☐ Transfer each batch of chips to the draining station and immediately sprinkle them with salt.

☐ In a small bowl, lightly toss the salmon with the truffle oil and add salt and pepper to taste.

☐ Spread the chips on a serving platter and spoon a tiny dollop of the salmon mixture into the center of each. Dab a small dot of crème fraîche on the salmon, and then lay a couple of chives on the crème fraîche. Sprinkle the lemon zest over the chips and serve!

MARISSA LIPPERT

Marissa devotes her energy and many talents to the promotion of nutrition and tasty food. She's the founder of Nourish (nourish-nyc.com), a firm that provides nutrition counseling and food consulting. The author of *The Cheater's Diet: The Sneaky Secrets to Losing Up to 20 Pounds in 8 Weeks Eating (and Drinking) Everything You Love* (Plume), Marissa is also a prolific food writer and recipe developer who has contributed to *Bon Appétit Magazine*, *Real Simple Magazine*, and *The New York Times*, among other publications. Her latest enterprise is Nourish Kitchen + Table (nourishkitchentable.com), a Manhattan food shop and café that showcases her passion for seasonality and the beauty of simple food.

FAVORITE CHIP? Marissa believes that nothing beats a good salt-and-vinegar chip on the beach—except for maybe a sour-cream-and-onion chip, ridged obviously. "I may be a dietitian, but I'll never pass up Cool Ranch® Doritos®," she says with a wink.

PAN-FRIED DECADENCE

This recipe showcases pan-frying, the frugal way to cook with costly oils and luxurious fats. Pan-frying only requires about a quart of oil, so splurge on connoisseur-quality olive oil, avocado oil, and luxurious duck fat. Using an inch or less of oil means fewer chips can be fried per batch, but the process is a bit more relaxed than deep-oil frying.

Here I've called for duck fat, the most sumptuous fat on earth. Its deeply savory flavor is reminiscent of bacon, without the wood smoke. Being fried in duck fat is the highest station to which potato slices can aspire (and each chip is individually deserving of a crème fraîche dollop and a caviar crown). Chips cooked in chicken fat aren't a shabby second—they're just as fabulous. Using an extraordinary cooking medium calls for a deluxe spice blend, as well. For these chips, it's truffle salt, white pepper, and a blend of poultry spices.

HUNTING-GATHERING

Duck fat isn't as rare a bird to bag as you might imagine. Look for it at high-end grocers and specialty markets, such as Williams-Sonoma, or order it online at Dartagnan.com. If you choose the schmaltzy route, chicken fat can be found at markets with extensive Kosher foods sections. Empire Kosher Schmaltz is a popular brand, usually sold frozen. To get 1 cup of bacon drippings you'll have to fry about 2 pounds of bacon. Isn't that terrible? All that crunchy, delectable bacon!

INGREDIENTS

Hot water for soaking
1 1/2 pounds russet potatoes, scrubbed clean or peeled
2 tablespoons distilled vinegar
2 cups duck fat
2-3 cups vegetable oil, preferably peanut or safflower oil

SEASONING

3/4 teaspoon truffle salt or fine sea salt
1/2 teaspoon freshly ground black pepper
1/2 teaspoon ground white pepper
1/4 teaspoon dried thyme, crushed between fingers
1/8 teaspoon ground sage
A pinch of freshly grated nutmeg

Deluxe Frying Blends

Duck fat, chicken fat, and bacon drippings are flavor-packed enough to mix with high-heat vegetable oils, such as peanut or safflower, or with lard, to make delicious and durable frying blends. Mix 2 cups of duck or chicken fat with 2 or more cups of oil or lard. Bacon drippings are super-concentrated—1 cup will flavor 3 or more cups of oil or lard. (Bonus: If you save your oil, bacon drippings and peanut oil make the classic Southern-chicken-frying blend.) All the blends will stand several sessions of chip-making and general frying. Cool the oil and pour it through a fine mesh strainer fitted with a coffee filter. The oil can be stored in the refrigerator for up to 2 months and in the freezer for about 6 months.

METHOD

PREPARING THE POTATOES

☐ Fill a medium-sized mixing bowl with about 2 quarts of hot tap water. Cut the potatoes into thin, even slices—1/16 inch (a quarter's thickness) is ideal for thin chips, while 1/8 inch (two quarters) is good for thicker ones. Use a mandoline if you have one. As you cut, drop the slices into the hot water to prevent darkening.

☐ Drain and replace the water with more hot water and add the vinegar. Let the slices soak for at least 15 minutes.

☐ Drain the slices into a colander and rinse them under hot water until the water runs clear of starch. Spread the potato slices across a kitchen towel and pat them dry with another towel. Roll up the slices in the towel and gently press to blot.

FRYING

☐ Prepare a draining station near your cooktop by lining a baking sheet with paper towels or a paper bag. Place a cooling rack on top, laid upside down.

☐ In a small bowl, combine the truffle salt, black pepper, white pepper, thyme, sage, and nutmeg, and set it near the draining station.

☐ In a 12-inch heavy skillet or sturdy wok, add the duck fat and enough vegetable oil to bring the depth to 3/4 to 1 inch of oil. There should be an inch (and preferably more) of headspace above the oil. Over medium-high heat bring the oil temperature to about 350°F.

☐ Unroll the potato slices, turn the burner to high, and put just enough of the slices in the oil to make a single layer. Move and turn the slices using a slotted spoon or tongs until the bubbling stops, and they're golden brown—about 2 to 4 minutes depending on thickness. Transfer the chips to the blotting surface and immediately sprinkle them with some of the seasoning.

☐ Continue to fry the remaining slices, allowing the oil to return to 350°F and making room on the blotting surface for the next batch. Don't forget to add seasoning to the chips as they come out of the oil.

☐ The chips will get crisper as they cool, so wait a few minutes to serve them. Allow them to cool completely before storing them in an airtight container. They'll keep for a couple of weeks.

☐ If the chips get soft or you want to serve them warm, reheat them for 4 or 5 minutes in a 300°F oven.

BAKED CHIPS WITH MAPLE-BACON DRIZZLE

PREP TIME: 10 MINUTES | SOAKING TIME: 15 MINUTES | COOKING TIME: 45–60 MINUTES | MAKES 3–4 CUPS

It's true that a batch of baked chips doesn't produce the same generous yield offered by fried chips. Oven space is limited, and the slices shrink a lot. But on the plus side, baked potato chips cook up with a concentrated spud flavor. And they're denser than fried chips.

I think of baked potato chips as small-batch treats that can serve as sturdy platforms for toppings and garnishes. Prime examples: the wild salmon tartar and toppings Marissa Lippert adds to her Blue Chips (page 46) and the Maple-Bacon Drizzle that follows.

INGREDIENTS

Hot water for soaking
2 tablespoons distilled vinegar
1-1¹/₂ pounds potatoes, peeled or unpeeled and scrubbed
2 tablespoons olive oil
¹/₂ teaspoon kosher salt, plus more for seasoning

METHOD

☐ Preheat the oven to 325°F, with the racks positioned in the upper and lower thirds.

☐ Cover two baking sheets with parchment paper or silicone baking mats.

☐ Fill a mixing bowl with about 2 quarts of hot tap water. Cut the potatoes into thin, even slices about ¹/₁₆ inch thick (a quarter's thickness). Place the slices in the water as you work.

☐ Drain and replace the water with more hot water and add the vinegar. Let the slices soak for at least 15 minutes.

☐ Drain the slices into a colander and rinse them under hot running water. Spread the slices across a kitchen towel and pat them dry with another towel. Roll up the slices in the towel and gently press to blot.

☐ Spread the slices in a single layer on the baking sheets—it's okay if some edges slightly overlap. Bake the chips for 20 minutes and then flip them. Rotate the baking sheets and switch their positions in the oven.

☐ Bake the chips for 20 more minutes, flip them again, and rotate the baking pans. Continue baking the chips until they turn golden-brown and become crisp—not limp. Remove the ones that get done early. The remaining cooking time—it could be 10 or more minutes—will depend on thickness.

CHIP TIP: If your chips don't seem to be cooking evenly or are taking too long to crisp up, flip them more frequently and rotate the baking pans more often.

☐ As soon as the chips come out of the oven, sprinkle them with salt, if you like, and serve them with the Maple-Bacon Drizzle below.

☐ Baked chips get crisper as they cool, so wait 5 to 10 minutes before serving them. Allow the chips to cool completely before storing them in an airtight container. They'll keep for a couple of weeks at room temperature.

MAPLE-BACON DRIZZLE

MAKES ABOUT ¹/₂ CUP

My parents once (and only once) spent a whole day and night slowly simmering the bucket of maple sap my father had collected from their suburban, St. Albans, Vermont, maple trees. "It only made THIS MUCH!" my mother would say, pinching her fingers close together to indicate almost nothing. "Never tried anything like that again." But it was while they lived in Vermont that real maple syrup became the family favorite for trickling over biscuits, cornbread...and grits.

The following is actually a caramel sauce recipe in which bacon drippings are used instead of butter. Ponder that for a minute. Bacon-flavored caramel. Mmmm. I love this drizzle on sweet-potato chips and regular potato chips. And thinking outside the chip, try mixing Maple-Bacon Drizzle with an equal measure of oil and some lemon juice for a scrumptious salad dressing!

INGREDIENTS

- 1/2 pound thick-sliced, wood-smoked bacon, diced about 3/8 inch
- 2 tablespoons bacon drippings, reserved from frying
- 1/4 cup minced shallots
- 1/2 teaspoon freshly ground black pepper
- 1/2 teaspoon Coarse salt
- 1/4 cup apple-cider vinegar
- 3/4 cup maple syrup, the real stuff, please
  Freshly squeezed lemon juice
  Coarse salt

METHOD

☐ Into a medium-sized skillet or heavy saucepan over medium-high heat, add the diced bacon and stir to separate the pieces. Fry the bacon until it's deep brown and very crisp. Homemade bacon bits!

☐ In a small saucepan over medium heat, add the reserved bacon drippings, shallots, pepper, and salt. Sauté until the shallots just begin to color—about 2 minutes.

☐ Add the vinegar and cook until it's reduced by half. Then add the maple syrup and simmer 6 to 8 minutes, stirring often, until the mixture thickens. From time to time, dip in a soup spoon and watch how the liquid drips off the back. The mixture is ready when it drips more like syrup than water.

☐ Allow the drizzle to cool slightly before serving—it will become thicker.

☐ The recipe can be made up to 5 days ahead. You should store the bacon and syrup separately in the refrigerator. Reheat the drizzle for a few seconds in the microwave if it becomes too thick to pour.

TO SERVE

☐ Pour the warm maple drizzle over the chips and sprinkle on the bacon bits. Squeeze a little lemon juice on the chips and add a few pinches of chunky, coarse salt, Good to go!

GUEST CONTRIBUTOR

Todd Porter and Diane Cu (WhiteOnRiceCouple.com)

FRIED

FRITTES TURNED CHIPS

PREP TIME: 10 MINUTES | BLANCHING: 10 MINUTES | FIRST FRY: 10 MINUTES | FREEZING: 30 MINUTES–3+ HOURS

SECOND AND FRITTE FRYING: 20 MINUTES | MAKES 5–6 CUPS

These elegant and addictive frittes are transformed to take on a crispy-crunchy potato-chip texture. Serve them sprinkled with freshly grated Parmigiano Reggiano and chopped Italian parsley, or have fun with the seasonings of your choice.

This 4-stage preparation follows a scientific process for making perfect, super-crisp fries and frittes. Because these particular frittes are sliced very, very thinly, they transform into stick-style potato chips. Don't be intimidated by this recipe. It's quite simple, and each cooking step is quick (2 minutes or less).

Here's what happens. The first step, *Blanching*, removes sugar and starch. *First Fry* then removes moisture from the potatoes, and *Freezing* them afterward breaks the cell structure, so that they release a good deal of water during *Second Fry*. *Fritte Fry*, the final, gratifying step, turns the chips a rich golden-bronze and makes them delightfully crispy.

MAKE-AHEADS

The time that the chips spend in the freezer offers a great make-ahead point. Or you can hold the chips for a couple of hours after the Second Fry and drop them into oil when your guests arrive.

INGREDIENTS

- 2 pounds (about 4 large) Russet potatoes, peeled and cut into 3/16-inch thick matchsticks
- 2 tablespoons distilled white vinegar
- 2 tablespoons sugar
- 2 tablespoons kosher or sea salt, plus more for seasoning
  Canola, peanut, or grape-seed oil, for frying
  Fresh cracked black pepper, to taste
  Freshly grated Parmigiano Reggiano, for garnish
  Minced Italian parsley, for garnish

  Note: Once peeled, the raw potatoes should be submerged in warm water throughout their preparation.

BLANCHING

❑ Pour about 2 quarts of water into a large pot set over high heat. Stir in the vinegar, sugar, and 2 tablespoons of the salt, and bring the water to a rolling boil. Add the potato sticks, return the water to a boil, and cook for 2 minutes (total time in the water should be 7 to 8 minutes).

❑ Drain the potatoes and spread them on a towel-lined baking sheet or a cooling rack. Let them air dry for 5 to 10 minutes.

FIRST FRY

☐ Prepare a draining surface near your cooktop by lining a baking sheet with paper towels or a paper bag. Place a cooling rack on top, laid upside down.

☐ Pour $1^{1}/_{2}$ to 2 inches of oil into a wide, heavy pot or wok. There should be at least 2 inches of headspace above the oil or 3 inches of rim showing around the wok. Over high heat, bring the oil to 400°F.

☐ Working in 4 batches, add $^{1}/_{4}$ of the potato sticks to the oil and cook them for 1 minute, stirring and moving the potatoes so they don't stick. Transfer the potatoes to the draining surface with a wire-mesh spider. Allow the oil to return to 400°F, and fry the remaining potatoes.

FREEZING

☐ When they're cool enough to handle, spread the sticks on a couple of plates or a baking pan that will fit in your freezer. They should cool for at least 30 minutes. For the best results, allow them to freeze hard for about 2 hours or even overnight.

CHIP TIP: This is a good make-ahead stage: the potatoes can be stored in freezer bags for about 3 months. They're easy to separate even after they're seemingly frozen into a block.

SECOND FRY

☐ Replace the paper in your draining station.

☐ Bring the oil to 400°F over high heat and add $^{1}/_{4}$ of the potato sticks, immediately moving and turning them. Cook the sticks until they turn a pale golden-brown (for about $1^{1}/_{2}$ minutes), and transfer them to the draining station. Don't overcook them. They'll resemble almost-crisp French fries. Continue frying the remaining sticks. At this stage, you can hold them at room temperature for about 2 hours.

FRITTE FRY!

☐ Replace the paper in the draining station, and set your seasonings—salt, pepper, Parmigiano Reggiano, and parsley—nearby, if using.

☐ Return the oil to 400°F and fry the chips in 4 batches again, this time until they're a deep golden-bronze and very, very crisp—this should take between 1 to $1^{1}/_{2}$ minutes. Transfer the frittes to the draining station, and season them immediately. Continue frying the remaining potatoes, allowing the oil to return to 400°F and making room on the draining station.

☐ Serve the frittes warm or at room temperature with the aioli on the side. If you're not going to serve them immediately, you can keep them warm and crisp in a 200°F oven on a wire rack set over a baking sheet.

☐ The frittes store very well for about a week in an airtight container. Just make sure you let them cool completely before closing them up.

AIOLI
MAKES $^{1}/_{2}$ CUP

INGREDIENTS

$^{1}/_{2}$ cup mayonnaise
  1 clove garlic, crushed or minced
    Zest of one medium lemon
  2 tablespoons minced Italian parsley
$^{1}/_{2}$ teaspoon Dijon mustard
    Freshly ground black pepper, to taste

METHOD

☐ Combine all of the ingredients. Store the aioli in an airtight container in the refrigerator until ready to serve.

DIANE CU AND TODD PORTER

This creative couple could be classified as food maestros. They're professional food photographers, stylists, and film producers, as well as the masterminds behind the widely acclaimed blog **WhiteOnRiceCouple**. com, which provides a window into their world of cooking, gardening, entertaining, and traveling.

Todd and Diane have been featured in *Food & Wine Magazine* (with several recipes on foodandwine.com), *Sunset Magazine*, and on The Cooking Channel. Their professional clients include Whole Foods®, KitchenAid, and Williams-Sonoma®. Todd and Diane are also the authors of *Bountiful: Recipes Inspired by Our Garden* (Stewart, Tabori & Chang), a treasure trove of photos and excellent recipes harvested from their own 1/4-acre Garden of Eden in Southern California.

FAVORITE CHIP? "Salt and pepper is always our favorite," Todd says, "particularly if the potato chip itself is great." Todd and Diane also like rosemary-flavored chips. They admit that their favorite time to eat chips is while enjoying the adult beverages they make from their cocktail-named citrus trees. "Our Margarita Tree is a Mexican lime tree, the Salty Chihuahua Tree is a grapefruit tree, and the Sidecar Tree is a Eureka lemon," Diane explains. "Yes," Todd adds, "we love to drink."

Potato Chip History

According to a colorful (urban) legend, George Crum invented the potato chip in 1853 at Moon's Lake Lodge in Saratoga Springs, New York. The catalyst for his creation was Cornelius Vanderbilt, who, as a persnickety diner, returned limp potatoes to the Lodge's kitchen to be made crispier and saltier. Crum was incensed. He vengefully sliced a batch of potatoes so that they were paper-thin, fried the slices to a crisp, doused them with salt, and plunked them down in front of ol' Corny. They made Vanderbilt smile (photographs prove this particularly doubtful). Success! Crum named his new culinary creation Saratoga Chips and put them in the center of every table.

Now for the true parts. Crum did indeed cook for Moon's Lodge, and Vanderbilt was a fan of his cooking. Also true: Moon's Lodge famously placed cones of Saratoga Chips at every table, as did other nearby resorts. The popularity of chips radiated outward, starting in Saratoga Springs, sweeping through New York State, and spreading to Pennsylvania, Ohio, and beyond. It's unlikely, however, that Crum originated Saratoga Chips. His (self-commissioned) biography makes no mention of them. Neither does his 1914 obituary. It's not clear how the legend of Crum's invention was spawned, but in 1940, it was written into a history of Saratoga Springs. In 1973, a chip-packaging manufacturer coined Cornelius Vanderbilt as the complainer in an ad campaign—no doubt because of his groovy muttonchop sideburns. Far out!

We all love a good invention story. But thinking that someone created the potato chip is like believing someone invented the boiled egg. For as long as there have been pots of boiling oil and thinly cut slices of food to drop into them, chipping of one kind or another has doubtless been taking place.

On the evidentiary level, cookbook references to thinly cut, crisply fried potatoes date back to Mary Randolph's *The Virginia Housewife of 1824*. Her recipe "To Fry Sliced Potato." [sic] Instructs

"*Peel large potatoes, slice them about a quarter inch thick, or cut them into shavings round and round, as you would peel a lemon; dry them well in a clean cloth, and fry them in lard or dripping. Take care that your fat and frying-pan are quite clean; put it on a quick fire, watch it, and as soon as the lard boils and is still, put in the slices of potato, and keep moving them till they are crisp; take them up, and lay them on a sieve; send them up with very little salt sprinkled on them.*"

Potato chips were first made and distributed on a large scale in 1895 in Cleveland, Ohio. That year, William Tappenden began delivering his home-made potato chips to area stores in a horse-drawn wagon. "Saratoga Chips" was painted on the side. Sales were good, so Tappenden geared up. He started using an automatic potato slicer and dedicated his barn to production—the first potato-chip factory.

By the turn of the century, chipping operations were showing up everywhere. Some of the brands we recognize today—Hanover Brand Potato Chips (now Utz®), Wise Delicatessen Company (now Wise®), and Barrett Potato Chip Company (eventually Lay's®)—had become large operations by the 1920s.

The *marcelled* chips created by Ballreich's Potato Chip Company of Tiffin, Ohio, in 1920 marked the debut of the wavy potato chip. The chip was inspired by the marcelled hairstyle so popular during that time—a do that featured corrugated waves crimped with a curling iron. Fast-forward 94 years, and Ballreich's is still cranking out marcelled chips.

In 1926, Laura Scudder invented the Bag of Potato Chips. Until then, chips were sold out of barrels (like crackers) or glass display cases. Each sale had to be scooped, weighed, and bagged, leaving stale and broken chips. Scudder, a potato-chip manufacturer in Monterey Park, California, paid her women employees to take home sheets of waxed paper and iron them into bags. The next day, the bags were filled with chips, ironed shut, and delivered to stores. Scudder also came up with another invention: the date-stamping of chips.

In the 1920s, the introduction of the mechanical potato peeler and the continuous fryer made possible potato-chip production on a massive scale (up until this point, all brands were kettle chips). By the 1930s, a potato-chip industry was fully in place, and many small kettle-chip producers couldn't compete.

H. W. Lay was in the right place at the right time when he signed on as a distributor for the Barrett Potato Chip Company in Atlanta, Georgia, in 1932. Lay drove around the South in a Model A Ford introducing his product to grocery stores, filling stations, cafeterias, and soda shops. He did well as a distributor. By 1936, he had 25 employees. Two years later, he purchased Barrett's manufacturing plants and rebranded the product as Lay's Brand Potato Chips. Lay built more manufacturing plants and bought smaller snack-food companies, eventually making Lay's the first national potato-chip brand. In 1961 Lay's merged with the Dallas-based Frito Company, maker of the bestselling non-potato snack chip, Fritos®. In 1966 that happy union produced Frito-Lay's Doritos® Brand tortilla chips—in taco flavor.

Making flavored chips—taco, or otherwise—wasn't possible until the 1950s. Until that time, packaged chips came unseasoned with a packet of salt inserted in each bag. In 1954, Joe "Spud" Murphy invented a way to add seasonings to chips during production at his Taytos chip factory in Dublin, Ireland. The factory's first flavored chip was Cheese & Onion, followed by Salt & Vinegar. (The first flavored chips in the United States were Barbecue and Sour Cream & Onion.) Chip manufacturers worldwide adopted Murphy's invention, making him a very wealthy man and securing his place in the Potato-Chip Pantheon, along with Crum, Tappenden, Scudder, and Lay.

SAGE SANDWICHED

These show-stopping chips consist of whole, fresh sage leaves embedded in golden, translucent potato medallions. Fancy as they look, they're pretty simple to put together. The process is kind of like making a sandwich. Don't limit yourself to sage for the herbal insert. Depending on your menu and the season, try sprigs of thyme, tarragon leaves, dill tips, or parsley leaves. They'll all be smashing—perfect as a snack or appetizer, side dish, or garnish.

Thinness is important here, so give your knife skills a practice run on an inferior potato, or pull out the mandoline. If you've been paying attention, you'll note that we're going counter to the starch-is-bad wisdom. Here, starch is the glue that brings everything together—so no rinsing allowed. The method is also different in that it calls for a weighted baking sheet to press the chips flat. Fun things to try!

HUNTING-GATHERING

Fresh, whole sage leaves are key. To match leaf size to potato size, you may have to buy extra and pluck out the just-rights. As for the too-bigs, too-smalls, and plain-uglies, fry them in hot oil until they're crisp, then crumble them, and use them to season chips (see Apple & Sage, page 106). Potato-wise, choose large Russets with smooth skins in shapely ovals.

INGREDIENTS

- 2 large (the bigger, the better) Russet potatoes, peeled
- 1/4 cup (1 stick) butter, melted (there may be some leftover)
- 20-25 perfect sage leaves
  White pepper or finely ground black pepper
  Kosher salt or sea salt

METHOD

☐ Preheat the oven to 400°F.

☐ Cover a large baking sheet with parchment paper or a silicone baking mat. Have ready another silicone baking mat or parchment paper cut to size. Also have on hand another baking sheet to stack on top.

☐ Cut the potatoes lengthwise into 1/16 inch-thick slices—or the thickness of a quarter. As you work, lay the slices out on a dry surface in the order they're cut. You want about 40 to 50 nice-sized slices.

☐ Lay a sage leaf in the center of every other slice, then cover those slices with their unadorned mates. Press each pair together and transfer them to the baking sheet in a single layer.

☐ Brush both sides of the slices with a generous amount of the butter, sprinkle them with salt and pepper, and cover them with a silicone baking mat or parchment paper. Place the baking sheet on top and then place a heavy ovenproof pan, or a clean brick, on top for weight.

☐ Bake for 15 minutes then uncover the chips. Turn the oven down to 350°F, turn the pan, and continue baking for another 10 to 20 minutes, depending on thickness. Check the chips often and remove the ones that get done early. The chips should turn a light golden-brown and be dry—not limp.

☐ Sprinkle the chips with more salt, if you like, and let them cool for 5 to 10 minutes before serving—they'll get crisper. Allow the chips to cool completely before storing them in an airtight container. They'll keep for 3 or 4 days.

COOKING OPTIONS

If you don't mind curly chips, go weightless. Bake the chips uncovered at 350°F for 15 to 25 minutes (depending on thickness), flipping them and turning the baking sheet after 10 minutes. Or just cut to the chase and pan-fry them in 3/4 to 1 inch of oil.

GUEST CONTRIBUTOR

Winnie Abramson (HealthyGreenKitchen.com)

BAKED

ZA'ATAR AND ALEPPO SWEET-POTATO CHIPS WITH COOL HUMMUS DIP

PREP TIME: 10 MINUTES | BAKING TIME: 1½ HOURS | MAKES 3–4 CUPS

Baked sweet-potato chips can be a little tricky to get right. If you slice the potatoes too thin, they'll brown too fast; if you slice them too thick, they'll never crisp up. For these reasons, I recommend using a mandoline to create uniform slices.

These sweet potato chips do best when baked in a low-temperature oven for about 90 minutes. I know that seems like an eternity but I promise they're worth the wait.

The spice-mix that coats the chips and the Cool Hummus are both inspired by the Middle East. For a slightly spicier chip, double the amount of the Aleppo pepper. For a zestier dip, use the greater amounts of lemon juice and garlic.

HUNTING-GATHERING

Aleppo pepper is a fruity, tomato-y chili that's a shade milder than crushed red pepper. It can be found in specialty markets or online. Substitute hot paprika, ancho chili, or cayenne (but be careful... it's hotter). Sumac powder, bright red and tangy tart, is used in middle eastern and Arab cuisine. Find it in gourmet and middle eastern markets, or online.

INGREDIENTS

- **2 large (about 1 pound) sweet potatoes, peeled**
- **2 tablespoons olive oil**
- **2 teaspoons za'atar (recipe follows)**
- **1/2 teaspoon Aleppo pepper, or substitute**
  1/8 teaspoon cayenne pepper to taste

METHOD

☐ Preheat the oven to 250°F, with racks positioned in the upper and lower thirds.

☐ Line two baking sheets with parchment paper or silicone baking mats.

☐ Cut the sweet potato into even, 1/16 or 1/8 inch slices (thinner slices will cook faster) and place

them in a medium bowl. Add the olive oil, za'atar, and Aleppo pepper, and toss to coat the potato slices.

☐ Arrange the seasoned slices on the baking sheets—they can touch but not overlap. Bake for about 45 minutes, and then rotate the baking sheets and return them to the oven on opposite racks. Bake for 20 minutes, then flip the chips and turn the pans again. From then on, check the chips every 10 minutes to make sure they don't overcook. They may take 20 to 40 more minutes, depending on their thickness.

☐ When they're done, the chips will turn a deep rusty-brown, and their edges will curl as they crisp up. Pull out the ones that are done early. The chips will firm up slightly as they cool. They don't store well, so eat them the same day.

ZA'ATAR

MAKES ABOUT 2 TABLESPOONS

INGREDIENTS

- **1 teaspoon dried oregano**
- **1 teaspoon dried thyme leaves**
- **1 teaspoon sumac**
- **1 teaspoon ground cumin**
- **1 teaspoon sesame seeds**
- **1/4 teaspoon freshly ground black pepper**
- **1/2 teaspoon kosher salt**

METHOD

☐ Combine all of the ingredients, and then store the mixture in an airtight container. For a richer blend, crush everything with a mortar and pestle for a minute, or pulse the ingredients in a food mill for 2 or 3 seconds.

COOL HUMMUS

PREP TIME: 5 MINUTES | MAKES ABOUT 1¹/₂ CUPS

INGREDIENTS

- 1 (15.5-ounce) can of chickpeas, preferably organic
- ¹/₄ cup plain organic yogurt
- ¹/₄ cup tahini
- 2-3 tablespoons freshly squeezed lemon juice
- 3-4 garlic cloves, peeled and cut in half

METHOD

☐ In a blender or food processor, combine the ingredients until smooth. Chill for at least 30 minutes before serving. The flavors blend better the longer the mixture is allowed to sit. The hummus can be stored for about 1 week.

WINNIE ABRAMSON

As part of a food-oriented family—her parents owned the famous New York City restaurant The Quilted Giraffe—Winnie Abramson has been cooking for as long as she can remember. A former naturopathic practitioner who is now a nutrition and food writer, Winnie is the author of *One Simple Change: Surprisingly Easy Ways to Transform Your Life* (Chronicle Books). Winnie has contributed recipes to *The Foodista Best of Food Blogs Cookbook* (Andrews McMeel); *The Food52 Cookbook* (William Morrow), and *Ramps: The Cookbook* (St. Lynn's Press). Her blog, HealthyGreenKitchen.com, is a swell landing-place for anyone interested in home cooking, holistic nutrition, and green living.

FAVORITE CHIP? Winnie is a fan of the renowned potato chip. And considering her fondness for spicy Aleppo peppers to season sweet potato chips, it's no surprise that she loves her potato chips picante, too. Jalapeno is the flavor that puts a smile on Winnie's face.

SOUR CREAM AND CHIVES BAKED POTATO CHIPS

PREP TIME: 40 MINUTES | DEHYDRATING TIME: 8–14 HOURS | MAKES ABOUT 6–8 CUPS

Making oh-WOW chips with a dehydrator can be challenging. Potato slices that spend 12 hours or more in the machine are transformed into... dehydrated potatoes. Exciting, huh? To make matters worse, the starch gets chewy and sets up like white glue. Moistening the slices with oil and doctoring them with seasonings will improve matters, but the chips will still have the texture of a communion wafer.

So here it is—the oh-WOW solution! This method utilizes the dehydrator's best qualities—concentrating and preserving the true, clean flavors of things. In this case it's the comforting flavor of a baked potato with lots of sour cream, butter, and chives.

INGREDIENTS

- 1 1/2 pounds baking potatoes, such as Russet, peeled and halved
- 1-1 1/2 cups water reserved from boiling potatoes (may not use all)
- 1/2 cup sour cream, full fat, please
- 2 tablespoons butter
- 1 tablespoon finely diced fresh chives (substitute 2 teaspoons freeze dried)
- 1 tablespoon finely chopped fresh parsley
- 1 teaspoon onion powder
- 1 teaspoon salt
- 1/2 teaspoon freshly ground black pepper, or more to taste

METHOD

☐ Place the potatoes in a saucepan, add just enough water to cover them, and bring them to a boil over high heat. Turn the heat to medium-low and simmer the potatoes until a knife easily pierces the center of one of them—about 15 to 20 minutes.

Drain the potatoes, reserving 1 1/2 cups of the potato water. You should have about 4 cups of cooked potatoes.

☐ In a large mixing bowl, add the potatoes, 1 cup of the reserved cooking water, the sour cream, butter, chives, parsley, onion powder, salt, and pepper. Using a potato masher, blend the ingredients until you have a smooth, slightly lumpy mixture. You want a smooth paste, so transfer the mixture to a food processor or use an immersion blender to finish. You've just made very smooth mashed potatoes.

☐ Line the dehydrator trays with non-stick dehydrator sheets or parchment paper (don't fret—it will peel right off). (The recipe should cover three 14 x 14-inch dehydrator trays.) Spread the mixture in a thin even layer with no holes or ridges, as though you're frosting a cake. An offset spatula would be helpful here. Set the dehydrator to 145° F and insert the trays.

☐ After about 6 hours, remove the trays. If the layers are dry enough, peel off the paper, flip the sheets, and return them to the dehydrator. Check them again in 6 to 8 hours. When they've turned a pale yellow-tan and are completely dry, they're done. They should be brittle and break easily. The total dehydrating time will depend on the type of machine you have and the humidity.

☐ At this point, you can break the sheets up into chip-sized bits and eat them, or place them under the broiler for 1 or 2 minutes and toast them. If toasting, don't take your eyes off of the chips once they start to show color—they can go from golden to burned in seconds. I prefer them toasted.

☐ Store the chips in an airtight container. They'll keep for about a week. If they get soft, crisp them up in a 300°F oven for 4 or 5 minutes.

FUSS-FREE MICROWAVE CHIPS

PREP TIME: 20 MINUTES | COOKING TIME: 30 MINUTES FOR ABOUT 4 BATCHES | MAKES ABOUT 2-3 CUPS

If you're looking for an easy way to get a potato-chip fix, then microwaving is the method for you. Microwave chippery is simple. Plus—a big plus—the veggies come out looking brighter than they would had they been baked or fried. So those gorgeous heirloom blue, purple, and red potatoes will hold on to more of their vibrancy. You can use this technique on all kinds of other veggies too—carrots, zucchini, beets, and of course, sweet potatoes.

You can add your own favorite flavors to the basic formula below. Instead of olive oil, try melted butter, nutty walnut oil, spicy chili oil, or go decadent and use bacon grease or chicken fat. And add seasonings such as rosemary, sage, thyme, and lemon zest.

If you're looking to go the healthy route, then add just a quick spritz of oil to the slices with a mister or cooking spray.

INGREDIENTS

Hot water, about 2 quarts
1 pound potatoes, any kind, peeled or scrubbed clean
2 teaspoons olive oil
1/2 teaspoon salt
Cooking spray
Seasonings of your choice, optional

METHOD

☐ Fill a mixing bowl with hot water and set it aside. Cut the potatoes into thin, even slices 1/8 to 1/16 inch thick.

☐ Immediately transfer the potato slices to the bowl of water and separate them. Allow them to soak for 10 to 15 minutes, then drain and rinse the slices under hot running water for a few seconds. Spread them out on a kitchen towel, roll it up, and press to blot them dry.

CHIP TIP: Only starchy vegetables such as potatoes, sweet potatoes, yucca, and taro need to be soaked. Skip this step for beets, carrots, squash, and non-starchy veggies.

☐ In a dry mixing bowl, add the oil and potato slices and toss until evenly coated. Add the salt and seasonings of your choice then toss again.

☐ Prepare the cooking surface—either the microwave's glass turntable or a microwave-safe platter—by misting it with oil or cooking spray. You only need to oil the surface once for all of the batches.

☐ Arrange the slices on the surface so that they're barely touching and cook them on high for 3 minutes. Turn the slices carefully—the plate and the slices will both get hot—and continue cooking in 1-minute intervals until the chips are golden. This can take up to 5 extra minutes, depending on how powerful your microwave oven is and the thickness of the slices. Remove the chips that get done first. Add more salt and seasoning, if you like.

☐ Microwave chips get crisper as they cool, so they're best served 3 or 4 minutes after cooking. Allow the chips to cool completely before storing them in an airtight container.

COOKING NOTES

If the chips don't brown evenly and come out with darker and lighter spots, it may be because the potatoes were older or previously refrigerated. Don't worry—they'll still taste delicious.

If your microwave seems to be cooking too fast or unevenly, turn the power down to 50% after you've turned the chips and add more time as needed.

Depending on the potatoes and your oven, you may be able to cook the chips without turning them. Give it a try.

JUST BEET IT

FRIED RAINBOW BEETS

PREP TIME 10 MINUTES | COOKING TIME 20 MINUTES | MAKES 3–4 CUPS

I first decided to try my hand at beet chips when I ended up with six bunches of perfect beet specimens that I'd gathered for a photo shoot. I'd made potato chips many times before and followed the same technique with the beets. They are quick and delicious.

HUNTING-GATHERING

All beets aren't beet colored. Thanks to the rediscovery of heirloom varieties (red and white banded chioggias, golden beets), a rainbow of colors is available, including shades of red ranging from pink to cheery crimson to purple. This fried-chip recipe is great for showing off the colors.

INGREDIENTS

3-4 large beets (about 1¹/₂–2 pounds),
     in a variety of colors
     Oil for frying
     Grainy sea salt

METHOD

☐ Prepare a draining station near your cooktop by lining a baking sheet with paper towels or a paper bag. Place a cooling rack on top, laid upside down. Make sure your salt is handy.

☐ Pour about 1¹/₂ to 2 inches of oil into a wide, heavy pot. There should be at least 2 inches of headspace above the oil.

☐ Prepare the beets by removing the root and stem ends and peeling them. Cut them into even (¹/₁₆-inch) slices. A mandoline will make the job easy and precise.

☐ Bring the oil to 325°F over high heat. Slide some of the beet slices into the oil, making sure you don't crowd the pot. The slices should bubble briskly on contact. Move and turn them constantly with a slotted spoon or spider. When the bubbling stops and the edges are curled— usually in 1 to 3 minutes, depending on thickness—the chips are done.

☐ Transfer the chips to the draining station and quickly sprinkle them with salt while they're still glistening.

☐ Continue to fry the remaining slices, allowing the oil to return to 325°F and making room on the draining station for the next batch. Don't forget to salt the chips as they come out of the oil.

☐ Serve the chips immediately or hold them for up to 6 hours uncovered at room temperature. To store the chips, allow them to cool and dry for at least an hour before transferring them to an airtight container. They can be stored for about 5 days.

PEPPERY DILL BEETS
WITH SOUTHERN DEVILLED-EGG DIP

PREP TIME: 15 MINUTES | BAKING TIME: 30 MINUTES PER BATCH | MAKES 3–4 CUPS

The ingredients here couldn't be simpler—it's the cooking method that's unique. Following my technique, you'll sandwich beet slices between matching baking sheets for the first 20 minutes of cooking—a process that results in vibrantly colored chips that are uniformly crunchy. You can skip this step, turning the chips instead midway through baking, and they'll still be delicious, but the chips will come out a bit darker and not quite as crunchy.

If you don't have perfectly matched baking sheets, don't fret—simply improvise with any pair of pans that can be pressed snuggly together. If you can pull together enough pan sets, go ahead and bake two batches of beet chips at a time.

HUNTING-GATHERING

Use purple varieties for baked beet chips. Yellow and golden varieties tend to darken and brown unattractively, while red beets actually brighten as they cook. Weird, huh?

INGREDIENTS

3-4 large red beets, about 1^1/$_2$–2 pounds

- 2 tablespoons oil
- 1 teaspoon freshly ground black pepper
- 1 teaspoon dried dill weed, or 2 teaspoons fresh dill, finely chopped
- ^{1}/$_2$ teaspoon kosher salt

METHOD

❑ Preheat the oven to 350°F, with the racks positioned in the upper and lower thirds.

❑ Line one of the two matching baking sheets with parchment paper or silicone baking mats. (You can bake more per batch if you have enough pans.)

❑ Prepare the beets by removing the root and stem ends. Cut the beets into even ^{1}/$_{16}$-inch-thick slices—about as thick as a quarter. A mandoline or food processor will help you make uniform slices.

❑ Transfer the beet slices to a mixing bowl, add the oil, pepper, dill, and salt, and then toss to coat.

❑ Arrange the beet slices in a single layer on the baking sheet with their edges just touching. Stack the matching baking sheet on top.

❑ Bake for 20 minutes, then remove the top baking sheet. The edges of the chips should look dry. Return the chips to the oven uncovered, turning the baking sheet in the opposite direction. Bake them for another 10 to 20 minutes, checking for doneness. The beets will curl and become lighter in color.

NOTE: The beet chips become crisper as they cool.

❑ If you like, sprinkle the chips with more salt when they come out of the oven. Then transfer them to a wide bowl or tray to cool.

SOUTHERN DEVILLED EGG DIP

COOKING TIME: 15 MINUTES | PREP TIME: 15 MINUTES
RESTING TIME: 1 HOUR OR MORE | MAKES ABOUT 1½ CUPS

Devilled eggs are always a good thing to bring to the party. But they're a bit tedious to make—think of all the boiling, peeling, halving, stuffing, and arranging they require. There's a simpler way to deliver the exact same flavor!: Mash everything up into a dip that's guaranteed to garner as much love as the oval appetizers themselves. The Southern style of this dip comes from a mustardy mix of sweet and tart, along with the twang of pimentos and sweet pickles. It's no secret that this is also a devilled egg-salad recipe, so spread it on some white bread for a tasty sandwich to go with your chips and dip.

This recipe is riding along next to Beet Chips, because beets and eggs are a stunningly perfect match of flavor and color. But the dip has an obvious affinity to the Southern-Style Hot Collard Chips (somebody give me a *y'all*!) on page 90, and paired with the Ionian Pita chips on page 149, it forms a proper lunch.

HUNTING-GATHERING
Where boiled eggs are concerned, you should go for the old. Really fresh eggs are hard to peel, so look for a carton with the oldest, closest, sell-by date.

INGREDIENTS

5 eggs
$1/4$ cup mayonnaise
$1/4$ cup (2 ounces) cream cheese, softened
1 tablespoon yellow mustard
1 tablespoon (1 lemon) freshly squeezed lemon juice
$1/2$ teaspoon kosher salt
2 teaspoons granulated sugar
1 teaspoon minced fresh dill weed
$1/4$ teaspoon celery seed, lightly crushed with fingers
$1/4$ teaspoon freshly ground black pepper
$1/4$ teaspoon turmeric
$1/8$ teaspoon garlic powder
$1/8$ teaspoon onion powder
$1/8$ teaspoon cayenne pepper, or to taste
$1/8$ teaspoon ascorbic or citric acid, optional (for tanginess)
2 tablespoons finely diced pimentos, blotted dry
1 tablespoon finely diced onion
1 tablespoon finely diced sweet pickle, well drained
Paprika for serving

METHOD

☐ Place the eggs in a saucepan large enough to hold them in a single layer. Fill the pan with enough cold water to cover the eggs by about 1 inch. Over medium heat bring the eggs to a full boil, then turn off the burner, cover the pan, and allow the eggs to sit for 15 minutes. Drain and cover them with cold water. When they're cool enough to handle, peel the eggs and chop them into rough chunks of about $1/2$ inch. Set the eggs aside.

☐ In a medium mixing bowl, combine the mayonnaise, cream cheese, mustard, lemon juice, salt, sugar, dill, celery seed, pepper, turmeric, garlic and onion powders, cayenne, and citric acid, if using. Blend until the mixture is smooth and creamy.

☐ Fold in the chopped eggs, and then use a pastry blender to chop and mash the mixture until it's an even mix of smooth and chunky resembling cottage cheese. You can also blend the mixture with a hand mixer.

☐ Fold in the pimentos, onion, and pickle. Taste the dip and adjust the seasoning, if necessary. If possible, refrigerate the dip for at least 1 hour before serving so that it can thicken and its flavors can blend. When you're ready to serve the dip, sprinkle it with paprika and more dill weed, if you like. After about a day, the dip will begin to get thin and somewhat runny, so eat it up sooner rather than later.

VARIATIONS

To shake things up, add 1 to 2 tablespoons of blue cheese, 3 to 4 slices of crumbled bacon, or $1/4$ cup of sharp cheddar cheese to the mix.

DOUBLE DILL CARROT AND PARSNIP RIBBONS

Carrots, parsnips, and dill are cousins in the plant world and kissing cousins in this recipe. These pretty orange-and-yellow sticks are seasoned with lots of zesty dill seed and lacy dill weed. The recipe follows the low-and-slow method to prevent the sweet carrots from browning too quickly. If you're impatient and don't mind some dark chips mixed in with the light, check out the alternate cooking method.

Carrots and parsnips have an affinity to rich Indian spices. Try a batch with tandoori seasoning or curry powder, or the warm spiciness of Ashley English's Ras el Hanout seasoning on page 127.

HUNTING-GATHERING

Select stout carrots and parsnips—the wider the better. To offset the significant shrinkage that will occur during the cooking process, use carrots and parsnips that are at least 1 inch wide, or your ribbons may look more like fettuccini. For a colorful presentation, track down some of the red, purple, or yellow heirloom carrots available at farmers' markets and some grocery stores.

INGREDIENTS

$^1/_2$-1 pound carrots, choose wide ones
$^1/_2$-1 pound parsnips, ditto that wide
   1 tablespoon walnut or olive oil
  $^1/_4$ teaspoon kosher salt
  $^1/_4$ teaspoon freshly ground black pepper
  $^1/_4$ teaspoon dill seed
 1-2 tablespoons fresh dill weed, loosely chopped (or $^1/_2$–1 teaspoon dried)

METHOD

☐ Preheat the oven to 225°F.

☐ Line two baking sheets with parchment paper or silicone baking mats.

☐ To make the slices, I recommend a Y-shaped vegetable peeler for this recipe. Lay the carrot or parsnip on a counter and hold it firmly at the stem end. Pull the peeler down the root in a steady, even motion, bearing down to make thicker shavings than you would for peeling.

HINT: When my Y-shaped peeler can't get at the last part of the root, I make a platform to perch it on out of the flat-sided handle of a large knife. This allows you to get every last ribbon. (See page 25.)

☐ Combine the oil and spices in a mixing bowl. Drop in the carrot and parsnip ribbons and toss them until they're evenly coated.

☐ Arrange the ribbons in straight lines on the baking sheets. They can touch and overlap slightly.

☐ Bake the ribbons for 30 minutes, then rotate the baking sheets and switch their positions in the oven. Bake for another 20 to 40 minutes (or more depending on thickness), until the color begins to deepen and some of the edges start to brown. Pluck out any ribbons that are done early.

☐ Sprinkle the chips with salt, if you like, as soon as they come out of the oven. Allow them to cool on the baking sheets for at least 10 minutes before serving. They'll get crisper as they cool.

ALTERNATE COOKING METHOD

Fry. Carrot chips fry up nicely in a couple of minutes in ¾ to 1 inch of oil heated to 350°F.

CELERIAC ATTACK WITH BLOODY MARY POWDER

PREP TIME: 15 MINUTES | COOKING TIME: 20 MINUTES | MAKES 6–8 CUPS

Celeriac, or celery root, is the Shrek of vegetables—hairy and lumpy on the outside, entirely lovely on the inside. Except for the rare specimen that can be dispatched with a vegetable peeler, removing a celery root's gnarly exterior calls for big gestures—like chopping off wide swathes of the skin with a large knife.

When the root is fried up as a chip, its celery-parsley flavor becomes marvelously concentrated—not the taste you expect from something that looks like a plain ol' potato chip. In a nod to the classic, celery-garnished beverage, homemade Bloody Mary Powder (see page 80) is used as a seasoning for these chips.

HUNTING-GATHERING

Look for firm, dry roots that feel dense rather than light. Green tops indicate a fresh specimen, but it's okay if they're topless. If you feel like being picky, go for roots with the least knottiness toward the bottom.

INGREDIENTS

1 1/2 **pounds celeriac**
1 **quart cold water**
1 **tablespoon vinegar**
   Neutral vegetable oil for frying
   Bloody Mary Powder, recipe follows on page 80

METHOD

PREPARE CELERY ROOT

☐ In a large bowl, combine the water and the vinegar and set the solution aside.

☐ Slice off the top and bottom of the celery root. (You may lose a lot of the bottom end if the knotty roots go deep.) Stand the celery root up and run a knife down the sides. Following the contour of the root, remove the peel in wide planes. If any deep

and dirty crevices remain, go back and dig them out with a paring knife as you would with a potato.

☐ Split large roots into halves or quarters lengthwise—whatever size is easiest to cut into chips.

☐ Cut very thin, even slices—1/16 inch (a quarter's thickness) is ideal for thin chips, or 1/8 inch (two quarters) for thicker. A mandoline or food processor will make this task much easier.

FRY THE CHIPS

☐ Prepare a draining station near your cooktop by lining a baking sheet with paper towels or a paper bag. Place a cooling rack on top, laid upside down. Make sure your salt and seasonings are nearby.

☐ Pour about 1 to 1 1/2 inches of oil into a wide, heavy pot. There should be at least 3 inches of headspace above the oil. Attach a thermometer to the pot. Over high heat, steadily bring the oil temperature to 350°F.

☐ Carefully drop the slices in, making sure you don't crowd the pot. The slices should immediately bubble. Keep them moving, turning them until the bubbling slows or stops—at this point they'll brown very quickly. Your total frying time should be 2 to 5 minutes, depending on thickness.

☐ Transfer the chips to the draining station and immediately sprinkle them with salt or the Bloody Mary Powder. Note: the chips will be floppy when they come out of the oil, but they'll harden quickly.

☐ Continue to fry the remaining slices, allowing the oil to return to 350°F and making room on the draining station for the next batch. Don't forget to add seasoning as the chips come out of the oil.

☐ Let the chips cool and crisp up 3 to 4 minutes before serving them. To store, let them cool completely and put them in an airtight container. They'll keep for 4 or 5 days.

BLOODY MARY POWDER

PREP TIME: 2 MINUTES | DRYING AND COOLING TIME:
ABOUT 90 MINUTES | MAKES 3 TO 4 TABLESPOONS

This recipe is fun. Recreating the flavor of a
Bloody Mary in powder form isn't complicated,
but it does require some dehydration time. For the
effort, you'll be rewarded with a spicy seasoning
for your celeriac chips and all kinds of other things
(try putting it around the rim of the drink that
inspired it). I usually double or triple the recipe.

INGREDIENTS

- 1/4 cup (2 ounces) tomato paste
- 2 teaspoons prepared horseradish
- 2 teaspoons freshly squeezed lemon juice
- 1 teaspoon kosher salt
- 1 teaspoon Worcestershire sauce
- 1/2 teaspoon hot pepper sauce, such as Tabasco
- 1/2 teaspoon sugar
- 1/4 teaspoon ascorbic or citric acid
- 1/4 teaspoon celery seed
- 1/4 teaspoon freshly ground black pepper
- 1/4 teaspoon chili powder
- 1/8 teaspoon garlic powder
- 1/8 teaspoon onion powder
- 1/2 teaspoon fine salt

METHOD

☐ Preheat the oven to 200°F and position a
rack in the center.

☐ Line a rimmed baking sheet with parchment
paper or a silicone baking mat.

☐ In a small bowl, combine the tomato paste,
horseradish, lemon juice, salt, Worcestershire
sauce, pepper sauce, sugar, ascorbic acid,
celery seed, black pepper, chili powder, and
garlic and onion powders.

FINISHING IN AN OVEN
☐ Spread the mixture across the baking sheet
in a thin, even layer using a spatula or offset
cake spatula.

☐ Bake the mixture for about 45 minutes. Then
turn the baking sheet and continue baking until
there are no sticky or damp spots—for about
30 minutes more.

☐ Allow the dried Bloody Mary seasoning to
cool completely on the baking sheet for 20 to
30 minutes—it will continue to dry as it cools.
Then peel the dried seasoning off the baking
sheet and grind it in a spice mill. You can also put
it in a sealable plastic bag and crush it between
your fingers. Grind and seal it up quickly before
it starts clumping.

☐ Add 1/2 teaspoon of fine salt to the Bloody Mary
Powder and store it in an airtight container.

FINISHING IN A DEHYDRATOR
☐ Cover a dehydrator tray with a non-stick liner
or parchment paper. Use a spatula or offset cake
spatula to spread the mixture across the tray in
a thin, even layer.

☐ Dehydrate the mixture at 145°F for 3 to 6 hours.
The time will vary depending on the model of your
dehydrator and the humidity.

☐ Grind the sheets into powder and add salt as
described above.

GUEST CONTRIBUTOR

Mark Owen (urbanfoodguy.com)

~ FRIED ~
# LOTUS WITH RED CURRY PEANUT DIP

PREP TIME: 15 MINUTES | COOKING TIME: 15 MINUTES | MAKES 3–4 CUPS

One of the things I like most about lotus-root chips is how easy they are to make. But unlike many things I tend to cook, locality and seasonality aren't what I'm thinking about when I make them. I'm an inquisitive cook, and lotus-root is an exotic vegetable with a unique texture and form. Since I live on the edge of Chinatown, I'm constantly tempted by the prevalence and coolness of lotus.

LOTUS FASCINATION

The lotus botanical profile goes like this: Lotus is a cousin of the water lily, and it grows like a weed in still waters throughout Asia. Every part of the plant is used in Asian cuisines—flowers, seeds, stems, and particularly the rhizomes that spread in huge networks underwater. These rhizomes are (misnamed) lotus root.

HUNTING-GATHERING

Asian markets are the best places to score lotus. Fresh lotus root has a smooth, creamy tan skin. It's easily bruised, leaving dark spots that eventually soften. Look for dry, smooth, firm lotus with no soft spots or mold. Lotus also comes whole and sliced in vacuum-sealed packs. The slices tend to be thick, so you'll need to cross-cut them to a chipable thickness. But, on the plus side, the slices are ready to cook—no soaking required.

INGREDIENTS

1 **pound fresh or packaged lotus root**
   Cold water to cover slices
1 **tablespoon lemon juice or vinegar**
   Oil for frying
   Grainy sea salt

METHOD

☐ Prepare a draining station near your cooktop by lining a baking sheet with paper towels or a paper bag. Place a cooling rack on top, laid upside down. Make sure your salt is handy.

☐ Pour about ½ to 1 inch of oil into a wide, heavy pot, skillet, or wok. There should be at least 2 inches of headspace above the oil or 3 inches of rim around the wok.

PREPARE THE LOTUS

☐ Remove the skin of the lotus root with a vegetable peeler, working into the recesses of the root as you would with a potato.

☐ Combine the water and lemon juice in a mixing bowl. Cut the lotus into even, ⅛ inch-thick slices (about as thick as two quarters). A mandoline will make this task easy and precise. You can make the chips really chunky, as thick as ¼ inch, but they'll take longer to cook. Place the slices in the water and allow them to soak for 5 to 10 minutes.

☐ Drain the water and turn the slices out onto a kitchen towel. Blot them dry, pressing down firmly. Keep the slices covered until you're ready to fry them.

NOTE: Soaking helps the chips to fry up to a light golden-brown. If you don't mind dark, chestnut-colored lotus chips, you can skip the soaking step. Simply blot the slices dry with a kitchen towel.

☐ If you're using packaged lotus slices, you just drain and blot them dry with a kitchen towel, pressing down firmly. If the slices are too thick, divide them horizontally with a wide, sharp knife, pressing down to hold them steady.

COOK THE CHIPS

☐ Bring the oil to 350°F over medium-high heat. Slide some of the lotus slices into the oil, making sure you don't crowd the pot. The slices should bubble briskly on contact. Move and turn them constantly with a slotted spoon or spider. When the bubbling stops and the chips turn a light golden-brown, they're done. Thin chips will take about 2 minutes, thicker ones, 5 to 6 minutes.

☐ Transfer the chips to the draining station and quickly sprinkle them with salt while they're still glistening.

☐ Continue to fry the remaining slices, allowing the oil to return to 350°F and making room on the draining station for the next batch. Don't forget to salt the chips as they come out of the oil.

☐ Lotus chips store well, for up to a week. Allow them to cool and dry for at least 45 minutes before storing them in an airtight container.

SEASONING SUGGESTION

Lotus-root chips pair up nicely with Chinese 5-spice powder. Mix ¼ teaspoon of 5-spice with 1 teaspoon salt and season the chips as soon as they come out of the oil.

RED CURRY PEANUT DIP

PREP TIME: 15 MINUTES | MAKES ABOUT 1 1/2 CUPS

Red Curry paste can pack a punch, but I like the contrast between the salty, crunchy lotus chips and this rich, spicy Thai staple. This dip does double-duty as a sauce that goes great with sticky rice.

INGREDIENTS

- 1/2 cup organic raw peanuts
- 1 tablespoon neutral-flavored oil (avoid olive oil)
- 1-2 teaspoons of red curry paste, according to taste
- 1 cup coconut milk
- 1-2 teaspoons palm sugar (brown sugar or white sugar works fine)
- 1 tablespoon freshly squeezed lime juice
- 2 teaspoons dark soy sauce (found in Asian markets), substitute regular soy sauce
- Salt, to taste

METHOD

❑ Preheat the oven to 350°F. Spread the peanuts on a rimmed baking pan and roast them for about 10 minutes. They should turn a few shades darker and become slightly fragrant.

❑ Let the roasted peanuts cool a bit and then transfer them to a food processor or blender. Grind them into a paste-like consistency, as smooth as possible.

❑ Add the oil to a medium saucepan over medium heat. When the oil is hot but not smoking, add the curry paste and whisk to combine with the oil for about 1 minute. Add the coconut milk, sugar, and the ground peanuts. Whisking constantly, bring the mixture to a boil. It will thicken up quite a bit.

❑ Once the mixture boils, remove the pan from the heat and stir in the lime juice and soy sauce. Taste the dip, and add salt and adjust the seasonings, if you like. Add a little water if it is too thick.

❑ Serve the dip slightly warmed or at room temperature.

MARK OWEN

A self-taught cook, Mark's 30-year food career includes service as a private chef and years of food styling at magazines such as *Bon Appétit*, *Food & Wine*, *Real Simple*, and *Martha Stewart's Everyday Food*, to name a few. He's also freelanced at the Food Network, working in the kitchen for Bobby Flay and Paula Deen. Now Mark's fulltime passion is **UrbanFoodGuy.com**, a blog focused on living sustainably in an urban environment. Measured out with information about buying and eating food that's sustainably and humanely raised, there are fabulous recipes and posts about travel and food experiences here and abroad. Mark and his husband, Neil, live in an apartment with an amazing kitchen in Manhattan's Lower East Side.

FAVORITE CHIP? BBQ all the way! As a rule Mark doesn't go for packaged foods, but he admits that a late night of bar-side elbow bending will stimulate a hankering for kettle Brand Potato chips. "Country Barbecue. They're organic." he declares, adding coyly, "Now you know all my darkest secrets!"

KALACIOUSNESS

At a farmers' market years ago, I overheard someone describe an amazing discovery—
a fabulous snack called kale chips. I thought, "Huh, that sounds different. I'll try it."
When I got around to making them the next summer, kale chips were everywhere—recipes
for them were appearing on food-related blogs and in magazines. Fast-forward to today,
and they're mainstream. You can find kale chips in the grocery store. The funny thing about
the bagged kale chips you can get at the grocery store is that they're EXPENSIVE.
You can make your own delicious chips at home for a fraction of the cost.

No wonder kale chips rocketed to the top. They're a righteously healthy snack that can be eaten with reckless abandon. They're simple to make, they eat like a potato chip, and they have a fraction of a potato chip's calories and carbs. Hallelujah!

THE LEAVES

I've experimented with a lot of different greens, and it turns out they all taste pretty similar as chips. Although the spicy-hot edge of mustard greens and arugula marginally carries through to a chip, it would be hard to identify their flavor if they were mixed in with other leaf chips. I've discovered, though, that there are distinctions between greens that are worth exploring: texture and shape.

Kale is at the top of the leaf-for-chip category, because its sturdy, low-moisture leaves are the perfect thickness. All kale varieties make great chips. I prefer dinosaur (also called Lacinato) kale because its flat leaves are the easiest kind to clean. Speaking of cleaning, if you really hate that chore, almost every grocery store sells bags of prewashed kale.

Collard greens, Swiss chard, beet greens, Brussels sprout leaves, and cabbage all make delicious chips, and they offer a variety of shapes to play with.

Avoid delicate greens with small, thin leaves—anything labeled Baby is off the list. These types of greens are quick to burn and come out too fragile.

These recipes are totally interchangeable depending on what's abundant or on hand.

A PERFECT KALE CHIP

A perfect kale chip is super crisp and green. The greener the chip, the brighter the flavor will be. But it takes heat to get to crunchy, and heat causes browning, which brings out bitterness. In the oven, kale leaves immediately bake to a bright green and then to olive. Then they go brown. Flavorwise, you want them to crisp in the green-to-olive range— a fun and delicious challenge. Here are a few different plans of attack.

DEHYDRATING

Hands down, the dehydrator yields the brightest green chip and cleanest kale flavor. Working in slow motion removes browning from the equation. But the process isn't quick. Dehydrating takes 4 to 12 hours, depending on the greens you're chipping, what's in the recipe, and how your dehydrator works. If you don't have a dehydrator and don't intend to buy one, let's move along to the oven.

BAKING

There are three ways to get baked kale chips— fast, medium, and slow. I recommend that you try the fast-oven method first. Make a test batch—just one pan of kale—to get a feel for the process and flavor. Whichever method you choose, don't pile cooked chips in a bowl after they come out of the oven or they may soften. Spread them out for 15 to 20 minutes, and they'll continue to dry and get crisper. Fast-cooked chips take longer to dry out than slow-cooked ones.

Fast oven (I want chips now!). At 350°F degrees, depending on the leaf and the coating, your batches will take 10 to 15 minutes. They'll have a toastier flavor with some browned edges guaranteed, the way some folks like them. Flip the chips and reposition the baking sheets halfway through, and then watch them like a hawk until they're finished. Fast-baked chips don't store well and get soggy in airtight containers.

Slow oven. With a setting of 225°F, this process is almost like dehydrating. It takes 30 minutes to 1 hour, depending on the seasoning and the leaf thickness. Heavily coated chips may take longer. While cooking, reposition the baking sheets and turn the chips. This method gives you the most control over cooking and doesn't require vigilant monitoring. The chips also store better because the moisture has been thoroughly removed.

Moderate oven. Set your oven to 275°F to 300°F, and—depending on the recipe—expect crunchy, bright-green chips in 15 to 25 minutes. Turn the greens and reposition the baking sheets halfway through. This is the method for you if you want quick-ish chips and a bit more control over cooking. These chips store well after they've been allowed to air-dry for about 1 hour.

PREPPING GREENS FOR CHIPS

Remove center stalks. With their centers aligned, stack 4 or 5 leaves, fold them over, and slice off their stalks. Slice each stack into segments that are 2 to 3 inches wide.

Clean the leaves. If your kale or other green has a bit of fresh-from-the-farm grittiness, vigorously swish the leaves around in a deep bowl or a stockpot filled with cold water. Leave the greens in the water for a minute and allow the dirt to settle, then drain. Repeat this process until nothing settles to the bottom.

Dry, dry, dry. This is an important step. Excess moisture on the leaves will cause the greens to steam and darken before they can dry and turn crisp. Moisture also prevents the oil (a crisping agent) from sticking. Running the pieces through a salad spinner (if you have one) is a great first step. Work in batches to remove as much water as possible. Towel blotting—actually making contact with the leaves—is the most effective final step. Lay the pieces on a kitchen towel and blot them with another towel.

FAST-OVEN
BAKED

SIMPLY KALE

PREP TIME: 10 MINUTES | BAKING TIME: 20 MINUTES

MAKES 4–5 CUPS

This is the universal seasoning and temperature for any green, whether it be kale, collard, or Brussels sprout. The timings may vary, but you're going to be closely watching these chips cook anyway.

INGREDIENTS

6-8 ounces kale, about 1 large bunch
  1 tablespoon olive oil
  2 teaspoons lemon juice
 1/4 teaspoon kosher salt

METHOD

☐ Prepare the kale as described in Prepping Greens for Chips on page 85.

☐ Preheat the oven to 350°F.

☐ Line two baking sheets (or more) with parchment paper or silicone baking mats.

☐ Place the kale pieces in a large mixing bowl and drizzle them with the oil and lemon juice. Toss to blend, using your hands to massage the coating over the kale. The leaves will wilt a bit.

☐ Arrange the kale pieces in a single layer on the baking sheets. Stretch out the leaves to flatten them as much as possible. You may need to bake them in batches, depending on how many baking sheets you use.

☐ Bake the pieces for 10 minutes, and then flip them with tongs, moving the drier outside pieces to the center. Turn the baking sheets and return them to the oven on opposite racks. Bake the chips for another 5 minutes and flip them again. Bake the chips for 5 to 10 minutes more, depending on thickness, until they're crisp. Keep a close watch on them—they'll burn in a matter of seconds. Ideally, they should come out green with a few toasty spots.

☐ As soon as they come out of the oven, sprinkle the chips with more salt, if you like. If you don't eat them immediately (and I defy you not to), allow them to sit for 20 to 30 minutes before transferring them to an airtight container. They'll keep for 2 or 3 days.

MODERATE-OVEN BAKED
+ DEHYDRATED

LEMON-PEPPER KALE CHIPS

PREP TIME: 15 MINUTES | BAKED CHIP TIME: 35 TO 40 MINUTES

DEHYDRATED CHIP TIME: 3–6 HOURS | MAKES 4–5 CUPS

INGREDIENTS

6-8 ounces kale, about 1 large bunch

  2 tablespoons olive oil
  1 tablespoon freshly squeezed lemon juice
  1 teaspoon grated lemon zest
 1/2 teaspoon (1 clove) freshly grated garlic
 1/2 teaspoon freshly ground black pepper
 1/4 teaspoon onion powder
 1/4 teaspoon kosher salt

METHOD

☐ Cut, clean, and dry the kale as described in Prepping Greens for Chips on page 85.

☐ In a very large mixing bowl, combine the olive oil, lemon juice, lemon zest, garlic, pepper, onion powder, and salt. Add the kale pieces and toss to evenly coat, using your fingers to massage the flavors onto every leaf. The leaves will wilt a bit.

FINISHING IN A MODERATE OVEN

☐ Preheat the oven to 275°F.

☐ Line two baking sheets (or more) with parchment paper or silicone baking mats.

☐ Arrange the kale pieces on the baking sheets in a single layer, spreading out the leaves to flatten them as much as possible. You may need to bake them in batches, depending on how many baking sheets you use.

☐ Bake the pieces for 20 minutes, and then stir and turn them, moving the drier outside pieces to the center. Turn the baking sheets and return them to the oven on opposite racks. Bake 10 more minutes and stir the pieces again. Continue baking,

watching the chips closely until they're dry and crisp—another 5 to 10 minutes (curly kale takes longer than flat-leaf varieties). Pluck out the ones that finish early.

FINISHING IN A DEHYDRATOR

Arrange the kale pieces on dehydrating trays in a single layer, spreading them out as much as possible. It's okay if they overlap a little—they're going to shrink.

Dehydrate the pieces at 145°F for 2 hours, then turn the leaves and rearrange the trays. Continue cooking them until they're dry and crisp—this should take an additional 1 to 4 hours depending on the model of your dehydrator and the humidity.

SLOW-OVEN BAKED
+ DEHYDRATED
# NACHO CHEESE KALE

PREP TIME: 25 MINUTES | BAKED CHIP TIME: 2–4 HOURS | DEHYDRATED CHIP TIME: 5–10 HOURS | MAKES 3–4 QUARTS

This recipe makes amazing chips that are totally addictive. There's a lot of taste-bud trickery going on here. Two super umami players—cashew nuts and nutritional yeast—are combined with tart lemon juice, salt, and a little oil to replicate the flavor—and the sensation of eating—cheese. A ripe red pepper goes into the mix for that Southwestern flavor. If you like, kick it up with cayenne pepper or smoky chipotles in adobo.

HUNTING-GATHERING

To make these chips, go with one of the curly-leaf kale varieties. They're the best at holding a thick coating of seasoning. You can use peanuts or almonds for this recipe, but I prefer buttery cashews because they soften to a velvety smoothness after soaking in water. You can use any sort of ripe red pepper that's in season—I like to use ripe red poblanos or pimentos when they're available.

INGREDIENTS

12 ounces kale, about 2 big bunches

$2/3$ cup (3.5 ounces) cashews, preferably raw and unsalted, soaked at least 30 minutes or overnight

$1/3$ cup diced red bell pepper

2 tablespoons water reserved from soaking cashews

2 tablespoons nutritional yeast

2 teaspoons honey or maple syrup

2 teaspoons freshly squeezed lemon juice

2 teaspoons oil

$1/2$ teaspoon (1 clove) finely minced garlic

$1/2$ teaspoon kosher salt

$1/4$ teaspoon finely ground black pepper
   Optional: $1/8$–$1/4$ teaspoon cayenne pepper or $1/2$–1 teaspoon diced chipotle in adobo

METHOD

☐ Prepare the kale as described in Prepping Greens for Chips on page 85.

☐ In a blender or food processor combine the cashews, red bell pepper, reserved cashew water, nutritional yeast, maple syrup, lemon juice, oil, garlic, salt, pepper, and cayenne or chipotle, if using. Blend in bursts for about 2 minutes, until the mixture is smooth and resembles Thousand Island dressing. You can also use a blender or submersion blender.

☐ Transfer the dry kale to a very large mixing bowl, dollop about half of the cashew paste over the leaves, and work it in with your fingers. As the leaves become coated, add more paste. Really lay the paste on thick—that's where the flavor is. You may have some cashew paste left over, depending on the curliness of your kale leaves.

FINISHING IN A SLOW OVEN

☐ Preheat the oven to 225°F.

☐ Line two baking sheets (or more) with parchment paper or silicone baking mats.

☐ Arrange the coated kale in a single layer on the baking sheets, spreading out the leaves to flatten them as much as possible. They can touch but not overlap. Fill as many sheets as your oven will accommodate and refrigerate any remaining kale for the next batch.

☐ Bake the leaves for 30 minutes, then carefully loosen and flip them. Turn the baking pans and return them to the oven on opposite racks. Flip and turn the pans at 30-minute intervals until the chips are done. It may take a total of 2 to 4 hours, and possibly more, for the leaves to dry and crisp. Remove the chips that finish first. The chips with the thickest coatings will take the longest.

☐ Allow the chips to cool and dry for at least an hour before storing them, refrigerated, in an airtight container. They'll keep for about a week.

FINISHING IN A DEHYDRATOR

☐ Cover the dehydrator trays with non-stick dehydrator sheets or parchment paper.

☐ Spread the kale on the trays in a single layer, spreading out large clumps as much as possible. The leaves can touch, but they shouldn't overlap.

☐ Dehydrate the leaves at 145°F for 2 hours and then carefully loosen and flip them. Rearrange the trays if necessary. Continue dehydrating, checking occasionally, until the chips are lightweight, super crisp, and the coating shows no signs of dampness. Depending on your model and the humidity, this could take another 3 to 8 hours. It's nearly impossible to over-dehydrate the chips—the drier they are, the better.

FAST-OVEN
BAKED
SOUTHERN-STYLE HOT COLLARDS

PREP TIME: 15 MINUTES | BAKING TIME: 20 MINUTES

MAKES 6–7 CUPS

Collard greens, with their large, sturdy, flat leaves, are perfect for chip-making, because they're easy to clean and shrink less than other greens. Young, tender collards cook like kale. I prefer large, older leaves. They have a more robust cabbage flavor and make thicker chips. They also take a few extra minutes to cook.

Bacon grease and chicken fat (schmaltz) might sound weird in this context, but the depth of flavor they impart to these chips is lip-smacking good. If that's not going to happen in your kitchen, use butter or oil, plus $1/4$ teaspoon toasted sesame oil.

HUNTING-GATHERING

The large amount of pepper sauce needed to carry the flavor to the finished chip dictates using a not-too-hot sauce. I use Texas Pete® or Original Louisiana® Hot Sauce, but there are lots of others. If heat's not your thing, substitute a 50/50 blend of ketchup and vinegar.

INGREDIENTS

10-12 ounces collard leaves,
about 10–12 large leaves
2 tablespoons mild-ish pepper sauce
1/2 teaspoon dry mustard
1/2 teaspoon freshly ground black pepper
1/2 teaspoon kosher salt
1/4 teaspoon onion powder
1 tablespoon oil
1 tablespoon bacon drippings or chicken fat,
melted and cooled slightly

METHOD

☐ Preheat the oven to 350°F, with the racks positioned in the upper and lower thirds.

☐ Line baking sheets with parchment paper or silicone baking mats. The recipe covers four 11 x 17-inch baking sheets, so prepare as many as will fit in your oven.

☐ Cut, clean, and dry the collards as described in Prepping Greens for Chips on page 85.

☐ In a very large mixing bowl, combine the pepper sauce, dry mustard, black pepper, salt, onion powder, and oil. Add the warm bacon drippings or chicken fat and blend with a whisk until emulsified.

☐ Add the collard pieces and toss until they're evenly coated. Massage the mixture in with your fingers, but be careful when you handle the pepper sauce.

☐ Place the coated collard leaves in a thin layer on the baking sheets. The pieces will overlap, but that's okay. They'll shrink as they cook.

☐ Bake the leaves for 10 minutes, then flip them with tongs. Rotate the baking pans and return them to the oven on opposite racks. Bake another 5 minutes and flip them again. Continue baking for 5 to 10 minutes until the collard chips look opaque and are dry. Watch the chips closely and remove the ones that bake quicker than the rest.

WASABI-PEANUT BRUSSELS SPROUT PETALS

PREP TIME: 30 MINUTES | BAKING TIME: 30 MINUTES | MAKES 3–4 CUPS

Pulling the leaves off of Brussels sprouts takes a bit of patience and perseverance, but trust me—it's worth it. The cute, crunchy bits eat like popcorn, and with their hot, wasabi bite and nutty flavor, they might not make it out of the kitchen.

This recipe calls for a moderate oven so that the moisture in the seasonings has time to dry before the chips brown. If you prefer quicker and simpler, follow the recipe for Simply Kale on page 87 but expect a few browner edges and some moist centers.

INGREDIENTS

2 pounds whole fresh Brussels sprouts,
  the larger the better

DRESSING

1 tablespoon freshly squeezed lemon juice
1 tablespoon wasabi paste (or 2 teaspoons wasabi
  powder mixed with 1 teaspoon cold water)
1 tablespoon peanut oil, or any neutral-flavor oil
1 teaspoon soy sauce
1/2 teaspoon freshly ground white or black pepper
1/2 teaspoon kosher salt
1/2 teaspoon toasted sesame oil
1/4 cup toasted or freeze-dried peanuts,
  crushed until the largest pieces are the
  size of whole peppercorns

METHOD

☐ Preheat the oven to 300°F, with the racks positioned in the upper and lower thirds.

☐ Line two baking sheets with parchment paper or silicone baking mats.

☐ In a large mixing bowl, combine the lemon juice, wasabi paste, peanut oil, soy sauce, pepper, salt, and sesame oil.

☐ With a paring knife, cut off a little of the stem end from the sprout, then pull off the leaves and drop them into the mixing bowl. Make a new cut across the bottom of the sprout every so often to loosen up more leaves. At the point where the effort versus the gain becomes ridiculous, set the resulting micro-sprouts aside for another use and move on.

☐ Toss the leaves in the seasoning mixture, salad style, until they're evenly coated. Transfer the leaves to the baking sheets and spread them out in a single layer.

☐ Bake the leaves for 15 minutes, then stir them around with kitchen tongs. Try to flip as many as possible—you don't have to be precise. Turn the baking pans and return them to the oven on opposite racks.

☐ Bake another 10 minutes and stir up the chips again. Continue baking, watching the chips very closely, until they're a little toasty but not burned— for another 5 to 10 minutes.

☐ Remove the chips from the oven and immediately sprinkle them with crushed peanuts and a little more salt, if you like. Serve the chips as-is, or drizzled with a few drops of fresh lemon just as they're being served.

☐ If they're cooked dry enough, Brussels-sprout chips will keep for 4 or 5 days. Allow them to air-dry for about 1 hour before storing them in an airtight container.

HERBED ZUCCHINI WITH REAL CUCUMBER RANCH DIP

PREP TIME: 10 MINUTES | BAKED CHIP TIME: ABOUT 1½ HOURS | DEHYDRATED CHIP TIME: 6–12 HOURS | MAKES 2–3 CUPS

Every summer my father planted a two-acre garden with way too many hills of squash. Predictably enough, those hills turned out squash like bubble machines make bubbles. The overabundance was frustrating for my waste-not mom (as it is for millions of people every summer), who was pushed into creative territories she did not love visiting. Between batches of stewed squash, she'd stuff and fry and grudgingly make casseroles. I wish she'd known about squash chips. My sisters and I would've eagerly munched our way through a few squash hills' worth of zucchini chips.

We're starting out here with a simple, basic seasoning blend, but the sky's the limit if you're into improvisation. Dill, garlic, curry, ranch, barbecue—squash chipping is a blank slate on which you can make a personal mark! A word of caution: Go easy on the salt. The slices shrink a lot, and their flavor becomes surprisingly concentrated.

HUNTING-GATHERING

This is the rare squash recipe that takes well to large, almost overripe squash. As long as the marrow is tight and not yet stringy, the large, developed seeds add an interesting texture and flavor to your chips. Any large, straight yellow squash or pattypan squash would work just as well as zucchini with this recipe.

INGREDIENTS

- 1½ pounds zucchini squash (3 large squash)
- 1-2 tablespoons olive oil, or a generous application of olive-oil cooking spray
- ¼ teaspoon kosher salt
- ¼ teaspoon freshly ground black pepper
- ½ teaspoon dried oregano
- ⅛ teaspoon onion powder
- ⅛ teaspoon whole celery seed, crushed between your fingers
  Pinch of citric acid, optional

METHOD

☐ Remove the stem and root ends, and cut the squash into even, ⅛ inch-thick slices—about as thick as two stacked quarters. Don't go any thinner than that or the chips will be too delicate. A mandoline makes uniform slices. If the squash is small, cut elongated diagonal slices.

☐ Sandwich the slices between kitchen towels or paper towels and gently press to blot out moisture. Leave them in the towels to dry for a while—30 minutes is ideal if you have the time.

☐ In a small bowl, combine the salt, black pepper, oregano, onion powder, celery seed, and citric acid, if using. Set the mixture aside.

FINISHING IN AN OVEN

☐ Preheat the oven to 250°F, with the racks positioned in the upper and lower thirds.

☐ Line two baking sheets (or as many as will fit in your oven) with parchment paper or silicone baking mats.

☐ Arrange the slices in even rows on the baking sheets—it's okay for them to overlap a little. Brush or spray them with oil and sprinkle them with some of the seasoning blend. Flip the slices, spray or brush them with more oil, and sprinkle them with seasoning.

☐ Bake the slices for 1 hour and then flip them. Rotate the baking sheets and return them to the oven on opposite racks. Continue baking for 30 to 45 minutes, depending on thickness and moisture. The chips are done when they show no signs of sogginess and are a light golden-brown.

☐ Allow the chips to cool on the baking sheets. They'll get a bit crisper as they cool. They can be stored in an airtight container for 3 to 4 days. Let them air dry for about 45 minutes before storing them.

FINISHING IN A DEHYDRATOR

☐ Arrange the slices in single layers on the dehydrator trays. A lot of shrinkage will occur in the dehydrator, so it's okay to slightly overlap the slices, but by no more than about 1/4 inch. Spray or brush the slices with a light coating of oil and sprinkle them with the seasoning blend. Flip the slices, apply more oil, and sprinkle them with seasoning.

☐ If your dehydrator has a temperature control, set it to 145°F and dehydrate the chips until they're very crisp, with no sogginess. Depending on your machine and the water content and thickness of your chips, this could take 6 to 12 hours

☐ You can store dehydrated zucchini chips in an airtight container for up to two weeks.

☐ **Tart them up.** Add an edge to your dehydrated chips by adding 1 teaspoon of vinegar or pickle juice to the oil when you toss the slices.

REAL CUCUMBER RANCH DIP

PREP TIME: 15 MINUTES | RESTING TIME: 2 HOURS OR MORE

MAKES ABOUT 2 CUPS

Homemade ranch dip is the best. Don't get me wrong—I like the hopped-up flavor of ranch dip made from the packet, but if you have access to the fresh ingredients in this recipe, you'll be amazed by how bright and summery the home-made version turns out. It makes a dandy dressing too, of course.

INGREDIENTS

1/2 cup mayonnaise
1/2 cup sour cream
1/4 cup (2 ounces) cream cheese, warmed
 3 tablespoons (1 lemon) freshly squeezed lemon juice
 1 tablespoon dried buttermilk powder, optional for richer flavor
 2 tablespoons coarsely grated cucumber, squeezed dry
 2 tablespoons finely chopped scallions, whites and greens
 1 tablespoon finely chopped parsley
 1 tablespoon (heaping) finely chopped fresh dill
1 1/2 teaspoons sugar
3/4 teaspoon kosher salt
1/2 teaspoon freshly minced garlic
1/2 teaspoon onion powder
1/2 teaspoon freshly ground black pepper
1/4 teaspoon celery seed (crushed between fingers)
1/4 teaspoon garlic powder
 1 tablespoon finely chopped fresh chives (substitute 2 teaspoons dried)

METHOD

☐ In the bowl of a food processor or medium mixing bowl combine the mayonnaise, sour cream, and cream cheese until smooth, then blend in the lemon juice and buttermilk powder, if using. Add the drained cucumbers, scallions, parsley, dill, sugar, salt, garlic, onion powder, pepper, celery seed, and garlic powder. Process in short pulses until the dip turns slightly green (10 to 15 bursts), or use a hand blender to combine. Stir in the chives (do not process).

☐ Taste, and adjust the seasoning, if necessary. Refrigerate the dip for at least 2 hours before serving. The dip will thicken, and its flavors will meld over time, so the further ahead you can make it the better. Add a few splashes of water if it gets too thick. Real Cucumber Ranch Dip keeps for about 5 days in the refrigerator.

BUTTERNUT SQUASH WITH CRANBERRY TOPPINGS

PREP TIME: 15 MINUTES | BAKING TIME: 30 MINUTES | MAKES 2–3 CUPS

Flecked with cranberries, rosemary, and sage, these chips taste like fall to me. Their aroma is the essence of the holidays. The perfect seasonal snack for holiday gatherings or any time you want to fill your house with the cozy scent of autumn, these pumpkin-flavored rounds have a cranberry topping that goes on just before serving and can be doctored with extra rosemary. Parmesan cheese is a lovely addition, either sprinkled on before baking or added afterward with the toppings.

Par-boiling accelerates the moisture-releasing process, which is the key to crispiness, and allows you to cook the chips quickly at a high temperature.

HUNTING-GATHERING

You can use other winter squash for this recipe—kabocha, delicata, acorn—but I think the butternut squash was custom-designed for chip-making. Its neck section yields perfect rounds, and its sturdy, dense flesh makes it easy to handle. Look for a squash that has a long, straight neck and a small seed bulb on its end.

INGREDIENTS

$1^{1}/_{2}$ pounds (1 medium) butternut squash
2-3 tablespoons oil—walnut oil would be nice
2 teaspoons finely chopped fresh sage leaves (6–7 leaves)
$^{1}/_{2}$ teaspoon ground black pepper
$^{1}/_{2}$ teaspoon finely chopped fresh rosemary
$^{1}/_{2}$ teaspoon kosher salt
$^{1}/_{4}$ teaspoon ground white pepper
2 tablespoons finely chopped dried cranberries
1 tablespoon honey
$^{1}/_{2}$ teaspoon freshly squeezed lemon juice
Coarse salt, such as Celtic or Maldon sea salt
Fresh rosemary for garnish

METHOD

☐ Preheat your oven to 350°F, with the racks positioned in the upper and lower thirds.

☐ Line two baking sheets with parchment paper or silicone baking mats and spray or lightly brush them with some of the oil.

☐ To prepare the squash, remove about $^{1}/_{2}$ inch from the top and bottom. Divide it into two sections where the neck meets the seed bulb, then remove the skin with a sturdy vegetable peeler or a paring knife. If you plan to use the seed bulb, scoop out the seeds.

☐ Cut each section into even, $^{1}/_{8}$ inch slices, about as thick as two stacked quarters. A mandoline or food processor would be helpful here. If the flesh around the seed bulb is less than $^{1}/_{2}$ inch thick, save it for another use.

☐ In a wide pot or deep skillet, bring about 2 quarts of water to a boil. Place a bowl of ice water near your cooktop. Cook the squash in 2 batches, boiling each for $1^{1}/_{2}$ to 2 minutes. Don't overcook them or they'll break apart. Carefully scoop the slices into the ice water.

☐ Lay the slices on a kitchen towel and pat them completely dry.

☐ In a mixing bowl combine the sage, black pepper, rosemary, salt, and white pepper. Pour the oil into another bowl for brushing. Combine the cranberries, honey, and lemon juice and set the mixture aside.

☐ Arrange the slices in a single layer on the prepared baking sheets so that they're close but not touching. Brush them generously with the oil, flip and brush the other side, and then sprinkle them with some of the herb mixture.

Bake the slices for 15 minutes, flip them and sprinkle them with more of the seasoning, then rotate the baking pans and return them to the oven on opposite racks. Continue cooking the chips until they're a deep amber-brown and crisp—10 to 15 minutes longer, depending on thickness. Check the chips frequently—they can burn quickly—and remove the ones that finish early.

NOTE: The chips will get crisper as they cool.

☐ To serve, spread the chips on a platter and drizzle them with the cranberry topping, coarse salt, and fresh rosemary.

ALTERNATE COOKING METHOD

☐ Fry. Butternut squash chips fry up nicely in a couple of minutes in hot oil! Par-boil and dry the slices as described above, then follow the basic frying technique on page 32.

LUXURIOUS FUNGI CHIPS

MAKES 2–3 CUPS | PREP TIME: 20 MINUTES | BAKING TIME: 40–60 MINUTES PER BATCH

Mushroom chips were a surprise! I didn't expect the concentrated, almost meaty flavor that would result from the simple formula of mushrooms, olive oil, basic seasonings, and a low-and-slow bake. But here's the thing: Mushrooms are mostly water and therefore shrink. They shrink a lot. So if it's a lot of chips you need, move on to another recipe. But if you choose to continue on here, you'll discover that mushroom chips add a luxurious touch to appetizer spreads and serve as opulent garnishes for creamy soups, risottos, and salads.

HUNTING-GATHERING

Use the largest mushrooms you can get your hands on. Portabella and large button mushrooms are obvious choices and are pretty common in grocery stores. Exotic and familiar mushroom varieties are popping up more and more at farmers' markets— the best place to luck into meaty King Oyster mushrooms. My favorite spot for foraging mushrooms is in Asian markets, where I often find large specimens at exceptional prices.

INGREDIENTS

Cooking spray or oil for baking sheets
16-20 ounces mushrooms
Olive oil for brushing or misting, or olive-oil cooking spray
1 teaspoon freshly ground black pepper
$1/2$ teaspoon kosher salt
$1/4$ teaspoon garlic powder

METHOD

☐ Preheat the oven to 325°F, with the racks positioned in the upper and lower thirds.

☐ Line two rimmed baking sheets with parchment paper or silicone baking mats.

☐ In a small bowl, mix the salt, pepper, and garlic powder, and set the seasoning aside.

☐ Cut large mushrooms into even $1/8$-inch slices using a mandoline or a sharp knife with a wide blade. Arrange the slices on the baking sheets in a single layer, slightly overlapping some of the edges. Brush or spray the slices with oil and sprinkle on some of the seasoning. (Spraying is much easier than brushing!) Turn the slices— their edges should still overlap slightly—and apply more oil and seasoning.

☐ Bake two sheets of the mushrooms for 20 minutes. The mushrooms will shrink by half, so you can consolidate them onto one baking sheet and start another batch on the one that becomes free.

☐ Bake the chips for another 20 minutes, then turn them. Continue baking, checking every 5 minutes, until the chips look dry and the edges are crisp—for another 5 to 20 minutes, depending on thickness.

CRISPING HINT: It's okay if some of the chips end up with moist centers. They'll be no less wonderful. But if you insist on through-and-through crispness, turn off the oven and leave the chips in it for an hour. You can also place any offending chips on a plate lined with paper towels and microwave them for about 30 seconds. But be careful—they'll burn quickly.

☐ The chips are best eaten fresh out of the oven, but let them cool and crisp for a couple of minutes first.

Mushroom Profiles

Portabellas are easily sourced and really, really big. Fresh ones have smooth, silky caps and are not dried out. The cap's edge should curl back toward the stem. Flat, chipped edges indicate a past-its-prime chip candidate. You should cut portabellas into long strips, leaving on the stem.

Button mushrooms make good chips if you can find ones that are large enough. Look for the 2- to 3-inch ones that are often marketed as stuffing mushrooms. Cut them into strips, stems and all.

King Oyster mushrooms, also called King Trumpet mushrooms, are all about the stem. They look like cartoon creations. Their long, vase-like trunks are topped with tiny little caps. King Oysters can be huge too—4 to 5 inches tall, or larger. Cut them lengthwise into planks. Cooked, they have a meaty texture. Chips made from King Oysters can easily stand in for bacon.

APPLE CART

In a ranking of non-potato chips by popularity, apple chips come in just under kale. But apple chips were a favorite snack long before the kale-chip phenomenon. Here's an assortment of apple-chip possibilities cooked in all the ways chips are made—baked, fried, and dehydrated—and seasoned in the ways we like them: sweet, savory, and spicy. The recipes can also be made with your favorite variety of pear—one that's on the firm, less-ripe side.

DEHYDRATED

SPICED APPLE CHIPS

PREP TIME: 30 MINUTES | STEEPING TIME: 30 MINUTES

DEHYDRATING TIME: 6–12 HOURS | MAKES 6–7 CUPS

Flavor-wise, apple chips from the dehydrator are the cleanest, brightest way to go. The dehydration process slowly removes all of the moisture, leaving behind nothing but crisp apple flavor. Soaking the apples in a sugar-lemon juice syrup will give you snappier slices that won't turn dark. The spice blend here is straight from the apple-pie playbook, but you can take it in any direction. A little fresh rosemary and lemon zest would be very delicious, or pair the chips with Ashley English's Ras el Hanout seasoning (on page 128).

INGREDIENTS

3-4 apples (1-1½ pounds), such as Granny Smith, Gala, Pink Lady, or Rome

SYRUP
1½ cups granulated sugar
1¼ cups water
  ¼ cup (2 lemons) freshly squeezed lemon juice
  1 teaspoon pure vanilla extract

SEASONING
  1 tablespoon granulated sugar
  ¾ teaspoon ground cinnamon
  ¾ teaspoon ground ginger
  ¼ teaspoon freshly grated nutmeg
  ¼ teaspoon kosher salt
  ¼ teaspoon ground black pepper, optional

METHOD

☐ Make the syrup. In a saucepan combine the sugar, water, lemon juice, and vanilla extract. Bring the mixture to a low simmer over medium-high heat and slowly stir it for 2 to 3 minutes until the sugar is completely dissolved. Transfer the syrup to a wide mixing bowl and allow it to cool slightly (it can still be warm, just not boiling hot).

☐ Make the seasoning. In a small bowl combine the sugar, cinnamon, ginger, nutmeg, salt, and black pepper, if using.

☐ Peel the apples, or leave the peels on if the apples are organic. Core them if you must, but it's not necessary. Cut the apples crosswise into very thin and even slices, ideally ⅛ or 1/16 inch thick. Pick out and discard the seeds. Transfer the slices to the syrup as you cut them.

☐ Gently shake and rock the apple slices in the syrup. Allow them to sit for at least 30 minutes. Longer is better—1 hour or more is ideal. Occasionally tip the bowl from side to side to coat the slices with syrup.

☐ Drain the apple slices in a colander that's positioned over a bowl to catch the syrup. (Do not discard the syrup! You've created an exquisite elixir that can be used in cocktails and toddies or frozen into a sorbet!)

☐ Arrange the slices in single layers on the dehydrator trays. Allow the edges to touch—they'll shrink away from each other. Sprinkle a pinch of the spice blend in the center of each slice, or use a small mesh strainer to dust the slices broadly. There may be leftover spice blend.

☐ If your dehydrator has a temperature control, set it at 145°F. Dehydrate the chips until they're completely dry, possibly for 6 to 12 hours, depending on your model, chip thickness, water content, and humidity. The chips should be completely dry and crisp.

NOTE: Because apple chips harden as they cool, from time to time, you should pop a test chip in the freezer for a few seconds to see if it's crisp enough for you.

FRIED

APPLE & SAGE

PREP TIME: 15 MINUTES | COOKING TIME: 25 MINUTES

MAKES ABOUT 4 CUPS

This is an unusual variation on apple cookery. Frying apple slices creates a rich chip that's velvety with the oil it's cooked in. The savory flavor is that of apple-caramel, with a hint of fried pies. Theses chips are dusted with a vivid blend of crumbled fried sage, black pepper, and salt. For even more depth, try using a smoked salt.

Once you get started with this recipe, fry some extra sage leaves. Intensely flavored and oil-rich, crushed, fried sage is a seasoning in its own right, perfect on potato chips and sweet-potato chips. Outside of the chip realm, whole fried sage leaves are amazing on soups and salads, and a fantastic nibble for a cheese board. Call them Sage Chips!

HUNTING-GATHERING

To reduce the possibilities of over-browning and of the chips absorbing too much oil, choose under-ripe apples. If you can't find under-ripe apples in the grocery store, go for pears instead. Pears are typically sold when they're still green and firm.

INGREDIENTS

Oil for frying
2 large (about 1 pound) under-ripe apples, unpeeled if organic (can substitute under-ripe pears)
3/4 teaspoon freshly ground black pepper
1 teaspoon grainy salt, Celtic sea salt or smoked salt would be nice
15-20 fresh whole sage leaves, rinsed and blotted completely dry
Fine salt for initial seasoning

METHOD

☐ Pour 1/2 to 3/4 inch of oil into a heavy skillet. There should be about 1 1/2 inches of headspace above the oil. If you're using a wok, add enough oil so that there's about 1 1/2 to 2 inches of oil at the deepest part, leaving at least a 3-inch rim.

☐ Prepare a draining station for the apples near your cooktop by lining a baking sheet with a few layers of paper towels. For the sage, lay a paper towel over a plate for draining. Have your salt and pepper nearby.

☐ Cut the apples crosswise into even slices 1/16- to 1/8-inch thick. Pick out the seeds and spread the slices on a kitchen towel, overlapping them like playing cards so that you can easily "deal" them individually into the oil. Blot away as much moisture as possible.

MAKE THE SAGE SEASONING

☐ Mix the pepper and salt in a small bowl.

☐ Bring the oil to about 325°F over medium-high heat and fry the sage leaves. They fry quickly, in 3–5 seconds, so work with only 4 or 5 at a time. They should be very dry and delicate.

☐ Place the leaves on the paper towels to drain for a few seconds. As soon as they're cool enough to handle, crush 5 or 6 leaves into the salt-and-pepper mixture using your fingers. Set aside the seasoning blend and whole leaves for serving.

MAKE THE APPLE CHIPS

☐ Carefully place some of the apple slices in the oil, making sure you don't crowd the pan. The slices will bubble energetically at first! Move and turn the slices in the oil with kitchen tongs as they cook. Cooking will take 4 to 6 minutes, depending on thickness. They're done when their color is deep golden-brown and their edges are curly and a bit darker. Be careful—once the slices begin to color, they can burn in seconds.

NOTE: The chips become crisper as they cool.

☐ Transfer the chips to the draining station and immediately sprinkle them with a little of the fine salt.

☐ Continue to fry the remaining slices, allowing the oil to return to 325°F and making room on the draining station for the next batch. Don't forget to add the seasoning as the chips come out of the oil.

☐ Before serving, allow the apple chips to cool a bit and crisp up. Then spread them on a serving plate and sprinkle them with the sage-pepper-salt blend. Arrange the whole sage leaves around the chips. These chips are especially nice paired with a refreshing dip, such as Ashley English's Yogurt Dipping Sauce on page 128.

☐ Once they're cool, fried apple chips can be stored for about a week in an airtight container.

CRYSTAL PEARS

PREP TIME: 20 MINUTES : BAKING TIME: 2 1/2 HOURS | MAKES ABOUT 35–40 PIECES

Dessert chips? Of course! Crystallized pear chips are a delightful treat on their own, but these gem-like creations also carry the power to transform. On a cheese board, set a stack of crisp, sweet Crystal Pears between a sharp gorgonzola and a nutty Swiss. On the dessert cart, atop cupcakes and ice cream, Crystal Pears will glisten like jewels. And here's my best for last: The opulent yet simple pairing of Crystal Pears and Azteca Chocolate-Chili dip. The recipe follows on page 110.

Don't be tempted to hurry the process and crank up the heat. Going low-&-slow helps ensure that the pear chips come out bright yellow-gold. And save the syrup that remains once your pears are poached! It makes a delicious pear-and-ginger simple syrup for beverages and desserts and can serve as the start of a delectable sorbet.

HUNTING-GATHERING

For this recipe, I like the form and true pear flavor of green Bartletts, but you can use any pear variety. Select fruit that's under-ripe and use all of it—skin, core, and seeds. Go with three pears if you want to cull out the imperfect specimens, and four if you're cutting by hand.

INGREDIENTS

- 2 large, slightly under-ripe pears
- 2 cups sugar
- 2 cups water
- 12 thin slices of fresh ginger, peeled
- 1 lemon, halved

METHOD

☐ Preheat the oven to 200°F, with racks in the upper and lower thirds.

☐ Line two baking sheets with parchment paper or silicone baking mats.

MAKE THE SYRUP

☐ In a wide saucepan or a skillet over medium-high heat, combine the sugar and water. Bring the mixture to a boil and cook it for about 2 minutes.

☐ Add the ginger slices and continue boiling for 2 more minutes. Reduce the heat to low and allow the syrup and ginger to simmer while you prepare the pears.

PREPARE THE PEARS

☐ Cut each whole pear into very thin, uniform slices, preferably 1/16 inch thick—about as thick as a quarter. I cut mine lengthwise for the perfect pear profile. Squeeze the lemon over the slices to keep them from browning.

HINT: A mandoline makes it easier to produce uniform, intact slices. If you're winging it by hand, use a super–sharp, wide-blade knife for better control. I also suggest adding an extra pear to make up for slices that don't come out intact.

☐ Turn the burner to medium and bring the syrup to a low simmer. Working in 2 batches, add the pear slices to the syrup in one layer. Simmer for 2 minutes while spooning the syrup over the slices, and then remove the pan from the heat.

☐ Using a slotted spoon, transfer the pears from the pan to a plate. Then arrange the pears on the prepared baking sheets so that they're close but not touching. Poach and arrange the second batch of slices.

BAKE THE PEARS

☐ Prepare an area for the chips to cool, either on wire cooling racks or a parchment- or waxed-paper lined surface.

☐ Bake the slices for 90 minutes to 2 hours until they're dry to the touch and rigid when lifted up. Turn them with rubber-tipped tongs or a non-stick spatula. You may need to work some of them loose and peel them up.

❑ Return the chips to the oven, turning the baking pans and switching their positions in the oven. Bake until the chips are crisp and completely dry but not browned—for another 20 to 40 minutes, depending on their thickness.

NOTE: The chips harden as they cool, so send a test chip to the freezer for a minute to evaluate readiness.

❑ Transfer the chips to the wire rack or prepared surface to cool. They'll harden and crisp as they cool. Serve them at room temperature.

❑ You can make pear chips up to 3 days ahead. Store them in an airtight container between layers of waxed paper or parchment paper.

AZTECA CHOCOLATE-CHILI DIP

PREP TIME: 15 MINUTES | MAKES ABOUT 1 1/2 CUPS

Long before the Aztec and Mayan ruins were ruined, chocolate and chili were being combined to make beverages, porridges, and black moles—the spice pastes that still hang together with chocolate and chili. It took a few millennia for this Aztec flavor combo to go mainstream. But *ay, Dios mio*, how we've embraced the chili-spiked chocolate flavor bomb!

Here's a luxurious dip that's embarrassingly easy to assemble. Its sweet-on-spicy magic makes any fruit chip a unique dessert. Maybe try it with the Kerala-Style Plantain Chips (page 120) or the Round-the-World Coconut Chips (page 124). I like to pair sweet and savory. And there's an amazing thing that happens when potato chips and chocolate meet. Try it!

HUNTING-GATHERING

Ancho chili powder has a deep toasty flavor and a mild-to-medium heat. Look for it in specialty markets, Latin markets, or the ethnic-food section of your grocery store. Good substitutes are New Mexico or Anaheim chili powders. Absolutely DO NOT substitute the seasoning called chili powder—it contains cumin, oregano, garlic powder, and salt. If you come up short, cayenne pepper will deliver heat but not a lot of chili flavor.

Chocolate is the star here, so go for quality. Use chocolate bars or chips labeled dark or semi-sweet and extra-dark or bittersweet. Mexican chocolate has a rustic graininess and earthy flavor you might like. Absolutely avoid inexpensive brands of baking chocolate.

INGREDIENTS

- 1/2 **cup heavy cream**
- 1/4 **cup water**
- 2 **tablespoons granulated sugar**
- 2 **tablespoons cane syrup (substitute corn syrup or honey)**
- 1/2-1 **teaspoon ancho chili powder, or** 1/8–1/4 **teaspoon cayenne pepper**
- 1/2 **teaspoon pure vanilla extract, preferably Mexican**
- 1/4 **teaspoon kosher salt**
- 1/8 **teaspoon ground cinnamon**
- 8 **ounces good-quality chocolate, broken into bite-size bits (resist the urge to bite them)**

METHOD

❑ In a medium-size, heavy-bottomed saucepan, combine the heavy cream, water, sugar, cane syrup, chili powder, vanilla extract, salt and cinnamon. Bring the mixture to a simmer over medium heat, stirring frequently. When rapid bubbles appear around the edges of the mixture, remove the pan from the heat. Do not allow the mixture to boil.

☐ Add the chocolate pieces to the milk mixture, pressing them to the bottom of the pan. Allow the chocolate to melt undisturbed for 2 or 3 minutes. Then gently blend the chocolate and the milk with a whisk until the mixture is smooth and glossy. Wait a couple of minutes and then check the mixture's consistency—it should resemble honey or syrup. If it's too thick, stir in small amounts of hot (not cold!) water.

DIP TIP: **The heat of a chili takes a while to bloom. This is particularly true of cayenne. Taste the dip a few minutes after it's blended. If it's not spicy enough, add a little more chili and wait a couple of minutes before tasting and adjusting further. In this way you can slowly add more chili until you reach your sweet spot— umm, heat spot.**

☐ Serve the Azteca Chocolate-Chili Dip immediately, while it's still warm. It'll stay dip-able for about an hour at room temperature. Brief passes through the microwave (30 seconds should suffice) will make it smooth again. The dip will keep for about 3 weeks in the refrigerator. You can microwave it for 1 or 2 minutes to reheat it. The dip can be frozen for up to 3 months.

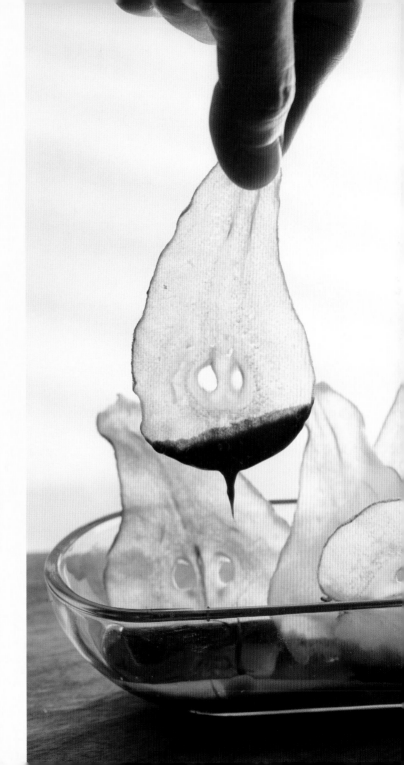

STRAWBERRY CHIPS

PREP TIME: 30 MINUTES | OVEN METHOD TIME: 2 HOURS | DEHYDRATOR METHOD TIME: 10–20 HOURS| MAKES ABOUT 50 CHIPS

You know that summer can't be far away when cheerful red strawberries start piling up in grocery stores and at farmers' markets. Before you start whipping up those shortcakes or cranking out the strawberry ice cream, pluck out the biggest specimens to make these ruby-red chips.

Strawberry chips are elegant on their own and even fancier when served alongside sweetened mascarpone or sour cream for dipping. If over-the-top is your style, plant crunchy strawberry chips on top of cupcakes or tuck them into dishes of ice cream!

If your oven goes lower than 200°F, consider going lower and cooking longer. Strawberry chips do exceptionally well in the dehydrator, where there's little danger of them turning brown due to exposure to heat.

HUNTING-GATHERING

Strawberries, being mostly water, shrink a lot as they slowly dehydrate. So try to get your hands on some really large ones. Choose firm berries that are almost under-ripe, preferably with solid cores. If you can't hand-select each berry, buy extras so you can sort through them. You have permission to send the small, misshapen, and really ripe ones directly to your mouth.

INGREDIENTS

        $1/2$ cup water
          1 cup sugar
    10-12 large berries, about $1/2$ pound, rinsed

PREPARING THE STRAWBERRIES

☐ In a small saucepan mix the water and sugar over high heat. Allow the mixture to boil for about 2 minutes, stirring constantly so that all the sugar is dissolved.

☐ Transfer the syrup to a bowl and place it in the refrigerator to cool for 20 to 30 minutes while you prepare the rest of the recipe.

☐ Remove the hull of each berry by cutting into its recesses (instead of slicing off the whole top). Cut the strawberries lengthwise into thin, uniform slices of about $1/8$ inch—as thick as 2 quarters.

OVEN METHOD

☐ Preheat the oven to 200°F, with racks positioned in the upper and lower thirds.

☐ Line a baking sheet with parchment paper or a silicone baking mat.

☐ Dip the strawberry slices into the cool syrup, coating both sides. Allow some syrup to drip away and place the slices on the baking sheet about $1/2$ inch apart.

☐ Bake the strawberry slices for 1 hour. Using something soft (I use bathroom tissue), gently blot away any large puddles of liquid. If you're cooking on parchment paper, it's best to flip the chips at this point to prevent them from adhering. Using a sharp-tined fork, lift the chips by their edges and gently flip them.

☐ Turn the baking sheet and continue baking until the chips are dry and stiff. You want them to remain bright red—they shouldn't brown. Depending on thickness and humidity, additional cooking time could be 1 hour or more.

HINT: Strawberry chips harden as they cool. You can check their progress by placing one on a cold metal surface or in the freezer for a few seconds. It'll harden into a crystalline chip if it's ready.

☐ Transfer the chips to a cool metal baking sheet and let them cool. If you're cooking on parchment paper, do this soon after they come out of the oven so they don't harden onto the paper.

☐ Flick off any sugar film that has formed around the edges of the chips, if you like. Strawberry chips should be stored between waxed paper in an airtight container.

DEHYDRATOR METHOD

☐ Cover the dehydrator trays with non-stick liners or parchment paper.

☐ Dip the strawberry slices into the cool syrup, coating both sides. Allow some syrup to drip away and place the slices on the dehydrator trays about 1/2 inch apart.

☐ Set the dehydrator on 145°F and dry the slices for about 6 hours. Blot away any liquid that puddles around the slices.

☐ When the chips are solid enough, remove the non-stick liners or parchment paper, and lay the chips directly on the mesh trays, flipping them over as you transfer them.

☐ Continue dehydrating the chips until they're completely dry and crystallized (see hint for testing doneness), usually in another 4 to 8 hours. The total time may be longer, depending on your dehydrator, the thickness of the slices, and the humidity.

☐ Flick off any sugar film that has formed around the edges of the chips, if you like.

STAR FRUIT

PREP TIME: 40 MINUTES | BAKING TIME: 1¹/₂–2 HOURS | MAKES 45–50 PIECES

The star fruit, also called carambola, is fascinating to behold. How could you not pick one up and admire its shiny, chartreuse skin and toy-like shape? I always do. And I love to smell the fruit. It has an undefined, fruity scent that reminds me of those icy treats in long plastic tubes that I loved as a kid.

Star-fruit chips make a nice, slightly indulgent tropical snack. Pair them with other extraordinary chips like Kerala-Style Plaintains on page 120 and Round-the-World Coconut on page 125 to create a dessert-chip medley or a tropical spread that you can serve along with slushy cocktails. Star-fruit chips, with their tart sweetness and cool shape, will take the starring role on ice cream, cakes, or a tropical cream pie.

HUNTING-GATHERING

Look for firm, shiny star fruits that are clear of blemishes. For this recipe you need slightly under-ripe fruit that's still showing some green along the ribs, tops, and bottoms. By comparison, a fully ripened star fruit is entirely yellow-gold with a good amount of browning along the edges of its ribs. Those are good raw but not sturdy enough for chipping.

INGREDIENTS

2-3 large, firm, slightly under-ripe star fruits
  2 cups sugar
  2 cups water
    Kosher or grainy sea salt, optional
    Ground cayenne pepper, optional

METHOD

☐ Preheat the oven to 200°F, with racks positioned in the upper and lower thirds.

☐ Line two baking sheets with parchment paper or silicone baking mats.

☐ Cut the star fruits into evenly thick slices— between $1/16$ and $1/8$ inch. A mandoline is helpful for achieving uniform slices, but a wide sharp knife will work fine.

☐ Combine the sugar and water in a medium saucepan or skillet and bring the mixture to a boil over medium-high heat. Cook it for 1 to 2 minutes and then remove it from the heat.

☐ Immediately add the star fruit slices to the syrup and coat them evenly by stirring and tipping the pan. Allow the fruit to steep in the syrup, uncovered, for 15 to 20 minutes or longer. Turn the slices once or twice while they soak.

☐ Transfer the slices to a strainer or colander placed over a bowl to catch the syrup. Allow the slices to drain for 10 to 15 minutes, or until the dripping stops.

NOTE: Save the syrup! Use it to flavor teas or cocktails, or as the base for a tropical sorbet.

☐ Arrange the drained star-fruit slices in a single layer on the baking sheets and remove the seeds. The slices can be close to each other but shouldn't touch. Sprinkle them with salt and a little cayenne pepper, if you like.

☐ Bake for about 45 minutes, then turn the baking sheets and return them to the oven on opposite racks. Continue baking for 35 to 40 minutes (or longer) until the chips are crisp and dry. The small ones will finish first, while the thicker slices will take longer.

NOTE: The chips harden when they cool. If you're not sure they're done, send a test chip to the fridge for a minute.

☐ Transfer the chips to a wire baking rack and let them harden and cool completely before serving. They can be stored for about 2 weeks in an airtight container at room temperature. Stack them between layers of parchment or waxed paper to prevent sticking.

VARIATION: For a tongue-tingling addition, add $1/4$ teaspoon of crushed Szechuan peppercorns to the water-sugar mixture. After straining, be sure to remove any peppercorns that cling to the star fruit.

DEHYDRATOR METHOD

You can finish star-fruit chips in the dehydrator by following the dehydrating method instructions for Strawberry Chips on page 112.

BANANAS AND PLANTAINS

The first two recipes in this section are similar and very simple. The first one describes the basic technique for frying banana chips, and the second involves plantains, turmeric, and an adventurous seasoning maneuver from India. You can exchange plantains for bananas for both recipes. Plantains are my top choice for frying because their starchy flesh makes the crispest chips imaginable. Bananas are the tastiest candidate for baked and dehydrated chips.

HUNTING-GATHERING

If you opt for bananas, select ones that are barely tinged with yellow. Plantains remain sturdy even when they're completely ripe, so you can choose from all-green to all-pale-yellow fruit. Predictably, yellower plantains yield sweeter chips, but their extra sugar makes for darker chips. If you're the experimental sort, use the smaller Asian and South American varieties that are available in the banana boutique of many grocery stores. The short, stout variety that's aptly named Red Banana works exceptionally well. Its sturdy flesh makes it ideal for cutting into lengthwise chips.

FRIED
FRIED BANANA CHIPS

PREP TIME: 5 MINUTES | FRYING TIME: 20 MINUTES

You can cut bananas into rounds for quick and easy handling, but I prefer to make diagonal cuts for larger oval chips. If you want to get dramatic and fancy, cut the bananas lengthwise—the long chips look cool served standing in a glass. Keeping long banana chips intact through cutting and frying can be a challenge, though, so if you choose to go this route, do a practice run with a couple of slices to work out your moves.

INGREDIENTS

2-3 green bananas or 1–2 plantains, about 1 1/2 pounds
Oil for frying
Salt
Curry powder, cayenne pepper, or other seasoning

METHOD

☐ Pour 1 1/2 to 2 inches of oil into a heavy pot or wok, allowing for at least 2 inches of headspace above the oil or 3 inches of rim around the wok. Attach a cooking thermometer.

☐ Prepare a draining station near your cooktop by lining a baking sheet with paper towels or a paper bag. Place a cooling rack on top, laid upside down. Place your seasonings nearby.

☐ Peel the bananas. If you're using plantains, see the peeling instructions and hints that follow in Kerala-style Plantains.

☐ Cut the bananas or plantains into even slices between 1/16 and 1/8 inch thick. Cut them into rounds or elongated diagonals, or into lengthwise slices from top to bottom.

☐ Heat the oil to 380°F over high heat.

HINT: Arrange the slices on dinner plates so that you can easily slide them into the oil.

☐ Transfer some of the slices to the hot oil without crowding the pot. For lengthwise chips, cradle 2 or 3 banana slices across a spatula for support and slide them carefully into the oil.

☐ Move and turn the banana slices carefully in the oil—try not to break them before they harden. Keep the chips moving as you watch for the bubbling to slow or stop. At that point, the chips will be hard and begin to color. They're ready when most of the chips are light yellow-gold—in 2 to 3 minutes.

☐ Transfer the chips to the draining station and sprinkle them with salt and seasoning, if you wish, while they're still glistening.

☐ Continue to fry the remaining slices, allowing the oil to return to 380°F and making room on the draining station for the next batch. Don't forget to salt and season the chips just as they come out of the oil.

FRIED
KERALA-STYLE PLANTAINS

PREP TIME: 10 MINUTES | SOAKING TIME: 30 MINUTES

FRYING TIME: 20 MINUTES | MAKES ABOUT 4 CUPS

Let's go on an adventurous trek for Indian street food. Our destination? A Kerala street market lined with huge woks of bubbling coconut oil next to head-high stacks of bananas and plantains still attached to branches. Cooks grab fistfuls of whole, peeled, turmeric-marinated plantains and slice them with wood and metal box graters directly into bubbling vats of oil. After a few turns of a paddle, in goes bright yellow turmeric water and up rises stormy columns of banana-coconut steam that wafts past your nose. In goes a pitchfork-sized slotted spoon and out comes a mound of the crispest, sweetest banana chips in the world.

Back in the kitchen, it's time to fry up some real chips! You may notice an unusual step in this recipe—the addition of water to hot oil. The maneuver calls for an extra degree of caution and preparedness, such as having safe access to the burner control if you need to turn the heat off. Cautionary measures aside, the oil will react pretty much as it does when any raw food is dropped in. It bubbles and steams for a few seconds, and then it stops. If you prefer to skip the water-seasoning maneuver, simply sprinkle salt and turmeric on your chips after they're done.

INGREDIENTS

2 plantains, about 1–1$\frac{1}{2}$ pounds
Oil for frying
Note: Coconut oil is traditional, flavorful, and very healthy. If using the required amount of it doesn't suit you, then add 3–4 tablespoons of it to regular oil. This will provide a good bit of flavor.

SOAKING SOLUTION
1 teaspoon ground turmeric
Water to cover

FLAVORING SOLUTION
3 tablespoons water
1 tablespoon salt
2 teaspoons sugar
2 teaspoons ground turmeric

METHOD

☐ Pour 1$\frac{1}{2}$ to 2 inches of oil into a heavy pot that's deep enough to provide at least 3 inches of headspace—this is very important because the oil will bubble up during the process. If you're using a wok (my preference), add enough oil so that there's about 1 to 1$\frac{1}{2}$ inches in the center, leaving 3–4 inches of rim. Attach a cooking thermometer.

☐ Prepare a draining station near your cooktop by lining a baking sheet with paper towels or a paper bag. Place a cooling rack on top, laid upside down. Have additional salt and turmeric nearby for seasoning.

☐ Peel the plantains by making 2 or 3 long slits from top to bottom through the skins. Try not to cut into the fruit itself. Peel the plantain—it's like a banana but harder. It helps to press your thumb under the peel to work it loose.

☐ Place the peeled plantains in a bowl just large enough to hold them. Sprinkle them with 1 teaspoon of turmeric and add enough water to cover. Swish and mix the turmeric, then allow the plantains to marinate for 30 minutes or more.

☐ In the meantime, combine the water, salt, sugar, and turmeric in a small bowl. Measure 2 teaspoons of the mixture into 4 smaller bowls—one for each batch to be fried. (You may not need all 4, but it's best to be prepared.) Set the bowls near your cooktop.

☐ Remove the plantains from the water and dry them completely with paper towels (a kitchen towel will stain). Cut the plantains into rounds or diagonals of an even thickness—between $1/16$ and $1/8$ inch. Use a mandoline if you have one. Arrange the slices in a single layer on 2 or 3 dinner plates and set them near the cooktop.

☐ Heat the oil to 380°F over high heat

☐ Carefully slide some of the plantain slices into the oil. Don't overcrowd the pot—you should work with about 2 layers of slices. The slices will bubble vigorously. Immediately begin stirring and turning the slices with a slotted spoon or spider.

☐ In 5 to 7 minutes the bubbling will slow or stop, and the chips will feel "plastic-y" and begin to turn golden-yellow. At this point, tip the pre-measured flavoring solution into the oil, and then step back from the steam for a second or two. It will pass quickly.

☐ Immediately resume stirring and turning the chips during the short time it takes for the oil to stop bubbling and for the chips to turn yellow-gold—in 1 or 2 minutes.

☐ Remove the chips with a slotted spoon, mesh strainer, or spider and transfer them to the draining station. If you like, sprinkle them with a little more salt and turmeric while they're still glistening with oil.

☐ Continue to fry the remaining plantain slices, allowing the oil to return to 380°F and making room on the draining station for the next batch.

BAKED + DEHYDRATED
HEALTHY BANANAS
PREP TIME: 10 MINUTES | BAKING TIME: 2 HOURS
DEHYDRATING TIME: 10–16 HOURS | MAKES ABOUT 4 CUPS

This is the simplest and healthiest route for making banana chips. A small amount of oil in the recipes prevents sticking and makes the chips crisper—and tastier. For baking, stick with under-ripe bananas. For dehydrating, go with borderline-ripe bananas.

INGREDIENTS

2-3 firm bananas (about $1^{1}/_{2}$ pounds), slightly under-ripe

2 tablespoons (1 lemon) freshly squeezed lemon juice

1-2 teaspoons oil for misting, or a good-quality cooking spray
Seasoning of your choice: curry powder, cayenne pepper, garam masala, and chili powder all pair nicely

OVEN METHOD

☐ Preheat the oven to 200°F, with the racks in the upper and lower thirds.

☐ Line two baking sheets with parchment paper or silicone baking mats.

☐ Add the lemon juice to a wide mixing bowl. Cut the bananas into rounds, angle them into ovals, or slice them into lengthwise strips. In thickness, the slices should be $1/16$ to $1/8$ inch. Drop them into the lemon juice as you work. Gently tip the bowl from side to side to coat the slices. Allow them to sit for 5 to 10 minutes.

☐ Arrange the slices closely on the baking sheets and mist them lightly with oil or cooking spray. Turn the slices and spray them with more oil. Sprinkle them with seasoning, if you like.

☐ Bake the slices for 45 minutes and then flip them—be careful, they may be very soft at this point. Turn the baking pans and switch their positions in the oven.

☐ Continue baking, repeating the flip-turn-repositioning of pans routine about every 30 minutes until the chips are dry, crisp, and light golden-brown. Total cooking time will be $1\frac{1}{2}$ to $2\frac{1}{2}$ hours, depending on ripeness, thickness, and how crisp you want your chips.

☐ Allow the banana chips to cool completely. They'll continue to harden and get crisper as they cool. Leave them uncovered for an hour before storing them in an airtight container. You can store them at room temperature for about a week.

DEHYDRATOR METHOD

☐ Apply a very light coating of oil to the dehydrator trays with a mister or cooking spray. If your dehydrator has a heat control, set it at medium or about 145°F.

☐ Add the lemon juice to a wide mixing bowl. Cut the bananas into $\frac{1}{16}$- to $\frac{1}{8}$-inch-thick slices—either into rounds or angled into ovals—and drop them into the lemon juice as you work. Gently tip the bowl from side to side to coat the slices with the juice. Allow them to sit for 5 to 10 minutes.

☐ Arrange the slices on the trays so that they're close but not touching, and sprinkle them with seasoning, if you like. Spray or mist the slices with a small amount of oil. This will prevent sticking and give you crisper chips.

☐ Dehydrate until you reach the chip crispness you prefer. (Some folks like theirs chewy. I like mine crackly crisp.) The total time may be 10 to 16 hours, depending on your dehydrator model and the thickness of the slices.

☐ Store the chips in an airtight container.

HARI CHUTNEY WITH PEANUTS

PREP TIME: 15 MINUTES | MAKES ABOUT 1 1/2 CUPS

Hari means green in Hindi, and hari chutney is one of the most beloved condiments in all of India. It's served as a dip with fried foods, breads, and raw vegetables. It's spread on sandwiches like mayonnaise. And it's used as a marinade and seasoning in itself. If you've eaten at an Indian restaurant, you've likely enjoyed this tart, fresh, slightly sweet condiment too.

There are many regional variations for green chutney—mint, yogurt, and coconut are typical additions—and most sub-continental versions are very spicy with many, many chilies added. The raw peanuts in this version add body without dulling the chutney's tanginess. And because no two Indian kitchens turn out the same hari chutney, feel free to adapt your own version of this recipe to be truly authentic.

HUNTING-GATHERING

Cilantro is hard to quantify. You'll need to buy 8 to 10 ounces. Depending on where you shop, that could equal 3 or 4 bunches. Just to be on the safe side, use the scales. **Serrano peppers** are moderately hot compared to the mild-to-medium heat of jalapeños. But heat levels are hard to predict from trip to trip to the pepper bin. Jalapeños can be substituted for the Serrano. If your supermarket doesn't offer raw peanuts, look for them at a market with bulk-food bins or at an Asian market. Raw almonds or raw cashews are fine stand-ins.

INGREDIENTS

- 3 cups (lightly packed) rinsed and chopped fresh cilantro, top stems included
- 3/4 cup skinless raw peanuts
- 1/2 cup roughly chopped scallions (white and green parts) or onion
- 1/4 cup (2 lemons) freshly squeezed lemon juice
- 2 teaspoons (about 1 large) seeded and chopped Serrano pepper, or more to taste
- 1 teaspoon coconut oil (substitute any oil)
- 1 teaspoon minced fresh ginger
- 1 teaspoon sugar
- 1 teaspoon (1–2 cloves) freshly minced garlic
- 1 teaspoon kosher salt, or to taste
- 1/2 teaspoon cumin seed, crushed
- 1/4 teaspoon coriander seed, crushed
- 7-8 whole black peppercorns, crushed
- 3-4 tablespoons cold water or lemon juice, as needed

METHOD

☐ Place all of the ingredients into the bowl of a food processor or blender and process them until they're smooth—for 1 minute or more. If the chutney is too thick, add some additional water or lemon juice (for a tangier flavor), and process it again until it takes on a pesto-like consistency. If it's not thick enough for your taste, process it with an additional 1/4 cup of peanuts. Then adjust the seasoning, adding more Serrano if you like.

☐ Hari Chutney has the brightest flavor when served the same day. It will keep for about 3 days in the refrigerator, but expect some darkening and fading of flavor. The best way to store the chutney and ensure that it retains its fresh flavor is to freeze it—it freezes magnificently for months. To thaw the chutney, microwave it for 30 seconds to 1 minute.

ROUND-THE-WORLD COCONUT

PREP TIME: 40 MINUTES | BAKING TIME: 10–20 MINUTESS | MAKES 3–4 CUPS

Coconut chips are ridiculously simple to make. The only hard part is getting past the shell to access the meat, or *copra*, as it's called. But if you're like me, you'll agree that any recipe that involves poking something with a screwdriver and then whacking it with a hammer is definitely worth a try. I always get excited when it comes time to crack a coconut.

Coconut chips are an everyday snack wherever coconuts grow. They tick all the boxes for a beloved nosh—they're sweet, salty, crunchy, and taste incredibly rich. They're also a healthy, clean food that shouldn't be limited to a snack bowl. Consider their potential as a garnish and an ingredient too. You can sprinkle coconut chips on a curry or a stir-fry or mix them into sautéed green beans. For dessert, make a chocolate cake and pile it high with curly coconut chips. Very dramatic! How about some toasted coconut-chip ice cream on the side?

The seasoning blends featured here were inspired by lands where coconuts are as common as water—India, Thailand, and the Caribbean. So release the tropical breezes, mix up the fruity cocktails, and prepare to munch your way to an exotic port....

HUNTING-GATHERING

Look for coconuts that have an even, brown-colored shell with no cracks or dark spots (evidence of seepage). The three eyes should be dry, not moist or moldy (further evidence of seepage). Most importantly, you should hear plenty of water sloshing around inside the shell. A dry coconut means there's dry flesh inside.

INGREDIENTS

1 fresh coconut
1 teaspoon kosher salt

SEASONING BLENDS

Chennai
1 teaspoon sugar
1 tablespoon Madras curry powder
1/8 teaspoon cayenne powder, optional

Lanna
1 teaspoon sugar
1 teaspoon lime juice
2-3 teaspoons Thai curry paste, such as massaman, green, or yellow

Caribe
1 teaspoon sugar
1/2 teaspoon freshly ground black pepper
1/2 teaspoon grated lime peel
1 tablespoon lime juice

METHOD

CRACKING AND SHAVING THE COCONUT

❑ Preheat the oven to 400°F.

❑ Use a screwdriver and hammer or a sturdy corkscrew to pierce one of the coconut's eyes. Push all the way through the meat, then drain all of the liquid. Save the coconut water for another use, or drink it while you make the chips. (Yum!)

❑ Place the coconut on a rimmed baking sheet and bake it for 10 to 15 minutes, or until cracks appear.

❑ Remove the coconut from the oven and let it sit until it's cool enough to handle. Wrap it in a towel and whack it with a hammer until you've made enough cracks to pull away some of the shell. Then, using a sturdy short knife (an oyster knife is ideal), pry away the rest of the meat.

☐ Divide the coconut into 4 or 5 large pieces, shave off the brown skin with a sturdy vegetable peeler, and then shave long, curling slices from the coconut chunks.

MAKING THE CHIPS

☐ If you're using a seasoning blend, combine its ingredients in a medium-sized mixing bowl. If you're using more than one blend, prepare them in separate bowls

☐ Gently toss the coconut slices in the seasoning until they're evenly coated.

☐ Divide the coconut curls between two baking sheets, spreading them into even layers. Sprinkle them with kosher salt and bake them for 3 to 4 minutes. Stir the chips, turning them as much as possible. Return them to the oven, turning the

baking pans and positioning them on opposite racks. Check the chips every 2 to 3 minutes, turning them often until they're done.

☐ Bake the chips until they're lightly golden with a tinge of brown around the edges. Plain or dry-seasoned chips take 10 to 12 minutes to toast, while those with wetter seasoning blends will take 15 to 20 minutes.

☐ Coconut chips can be stored in an airtight container at room temperature for a week or two. If your chips get soft, reheat them in a 350°F oven for a few minutes until they're crisp again.

GUEST CONTRIBUTOR

Ashley English (smallmeasure.com)

BAKED

BAKED RAS EL HANOUT APPLE CHIPS WITH YOGURT DIPPING SAUCE

PREP TIME: 15 MINUTES | BAKING AND DRYING TIME: 2$\frac{1}{2}$ HOURS | MAKES 30–45 CHIPS

INGREDIENTS

FOR THE CHIPS
2-3 large apples, washed and dried
   Nonstick cooking spray (I used coconut oil)
1/4 cup sugar
4 teaspoons Ras el Hanout (recipe follows)

FOR THE RAS EL HANOUT SEASONING
1 teaspoon black peppercorns
2 teaspoons coriander seeds
2 teaspoons cumin seeds
1 teaspoon cardamom seeds (from several
   green cardamom pods)
1 teaspoon fennel seeds
1 teaspoon ground cinnamon
1 teaspoon ground ginger
1 teaspoon smoky paprika
1 teaspoon ground turmeric
1/2 teaspoon ground allspice
1/2 teaspoon ground cloves
1/2 teaspoon salt

FOR THE YOGURT DIPPING SAUCE
1 cup Greek yogurt
   Zest of 1 orange
1 tablespoon honey
2 teaspoons Ras el Hanout (recipe follows)
1 teaspoon lemon juice

METHOD

MAKE THE RAS EL HANOUT
☐ Place the peppercorns and the coriander, cumin, cardamom, and fennel seeds in a heavy-bottomed pan such as an iron skillet. Dry-toast the seeds over low heat for 7 to 8 minutes, stirring occasionally until the seeds become fragrant and slightly browned. Remove the pan from the heat and transfer the seeds to a small bowl. Allow them to cool for about 5 minutes.

☐ Using a coffee grinder, food processor, or mortar and pestle, grind the toasted seeds to a powder. Use a fine strainer to separate the solids from the powder, shaking the powder into a small bowl. Discard or compost the solids.

☐ Add the cinnamon, ginger, smoked paprika, turmeric, allspice, cloves, and salt to the toasted spices and combine. **NOTE:** This recipe yields more Ras el Hanout than you'll need to make the apple chips and dip. Store the remaining portion in an airtight container out of direct sunlight and use it within 6 months.

☐ In a small bowl, combine 1/4 cup sugar and 4 teaspoons ras el hanout. Set the mixture aside.

MAKE THE CHIPS
☐ Preheat the oven to 250°F, with the racks positioned in the upper and lower thirds. Line two 12 x 17-inch baking sheets with parchment paper or silicone baking mats. Spray them generously with nonstick cooking spray and set them aside.

☐ Cut about 1/4 inch from the bottom of each apple. This will provide a flat, level surface for slicing. Using a mandoline, cut the apples into thin slices about 1/8 inch thick, placing them cut-side down on the slicer. If you don't have a mandoline, cut the apples into very thin slices with a large knife.

☐ Remove the apple seeds with a small pointy-tip knife. Arrange the apple slices evenly across the baking sheets—it's okay for the edges to touch.

☐ Sprinkle the chips with some of the sugar and the Ras el Hanout mixture. Flip the slices and sprinkle the other sides.

☐ Bake the slices for 1 hour and then flip the chips. Turn the baking sheets and switch their positions in the oven. Bake for an additional hour. Turn off the oven and leave the baking sheets in it for 30 minutes more.

☐ Remove the baking sheets from the oven. The chips will continue to crisp up as they cool.

☐ The apple chips are best served the day they're prepared, but they can be stored in an airtight container for about a week. Serve with the yogurt dipping sauce.

MAKE THE YOGURT DIPPING SAUCE
☐ Combine the yogurt, orange zest, honey, ras el hanout, and lemon juice. The sauce can be stored for 3 or 4 days.

ASHLEY ENGLISH

Ashley, her husband, and their young son Huxley—along with a menagerie of chickens, dogs, cats, and bees—homestead in Candler, North Carolina. Ashley is the author of *The Homemade Living* series, *A Year of Pies: A Seasonal Tour of Home Baked Pies* (all from Lark Books), *Handmade Gatherings: Recipes and Crafts for Seasonal Celebrations and Potluck Parties*, and *Quench: Handcrafted Beverages to Satisfy Every Taste and Occasion* (both from Roost Books). You can follow her adventures in homesteading on her blog, **smallmeasure.com**.

FAVORITE CHIP? Ashley's a can't-eat-just-one kinda gal. Other than her own apple chips or salted-root vegetable chips, she goes crazy for Salt & Black Pepper potato chips. And she declares that rosemary and lemon-zest potato chips are "finger-lickin' good!"

TOFU CHICHARONES WITH SRIRACHA POWDER

PREP TIME: 5 MINUTES | FRYING TIME: 15 MINUTES | MAKES ABOUT 6 CUPS (4–5 SERVINGS)

Here's something really different. Vegetarian chicharones. You heard right. Hardcore pork rind lovers and determined vegetarians can agree to agree that these are some mighty fine fried skins. This is an easy recipe with the added kick that it's super fun to make—in that magic-of-popcorn kind of way. The second they hit the oil, the pieces of dried tofu transform before your eyes, expanding in a dramatic puff of glory! And talk about crisp.

What Exactly Is Tofu Skin?

I was hoping you'd ask because I think it's pretty interesting. If you're the sort to dive in deep and try to make your own tofu skin, (or *yuba* as it's called in Japan), here's the process in a nutshell.

It all starts with a simmering pot of soymilk. If you've ever made hot chocolate from scratch, you know that when you stop stirring the simmering milk, a skin forms on top. And if you blow across the surface of the milk, that skin thickens and coagulates. The same thing happens to soymilk. As it simmers, air gets fanned across its surface and a skin forms that's periodically peeled off. This is tofu skin. Once it's pulled off, the dripping sheets are spread across bamboo mats or metal racks until it's thoroughly dried. The sheets of tofu skin are then cut up and packaged. Tofu skin is used like wontons to wrap morsels of food for dumplings and cut into strands to be used like noodles.

HUNTING-GATHERING

Tofu skin is easy to find at Asian markets (especially those specializing in Japanese, Chinese, and Vietnamese food), or you can order it online. It comes in a variety of shapes—curled, in sticks, and in flat, lasagna-like sheets. You want the flat sheets. If you have choices, pick the brand with the thickest skin because they make the "meatiest" chicharones.

INGREDIENTS

- 2-3 **ounces dried tofu skin sheets, the thicker the better (I use four 7 x 10-inch sheets)**
  Oil for frying
- 1 **tablespoon Sriracha Powder (the recipe follows on page 132)**
- 1/2 **teaspoon brown sugar**
- 1/4 **teaspoon fine sea salt**
- 1/8 **teaspoon garlic powder**
- 1/8 **teaspoon citric or ascorbic acid, optional**

METHOD

☐ Prepare a draining station near your cooktop by lining a baking sheet with paper towels or a paper bag. Place a cooling rack on top, laid upside-down.

☐ In a small bowl, combine the Sriracha Powder, brown sugar, salt, garlic powder, and citric acid, if using. Set the seasoning near the draining station.

☐ Pour about 1 1/2 inches of oil into a wide, heavy-bottomed pot or wok. There should be at least 2 inches of headspace above the oil or 3 inches of rim around the wok. Bring the oil temperature to 360°F over high heat.

☐ Break the tofu skin into pieces no wider than 2 inches. (They really do expand a lot!)

☐ Use a mesh strainer or slotted spoon to carefully lower 2 or 3 pieces into the oil—don't add too many, or they'll stick together. The pieces will bubble and sizzle dramatically as they puff up. Turn them with tongs or chopsticks as they cook. When they turn golden brown, they're done. Be ready to move quickly! They'll cook in seconds, and they easily scorch—more reasons to only cook a few at a time.

☐ Transfer the tofu chicharrones to the draining station and immediately sprinkle them with some of the Sriracha seasoning blend, to taste. Allow the

chips to cool before eating. Serve them with some extra seasoning for sprinkling.

☐ You can store chips for about a week in an airtight container at room temperature.

☐ Bonus: Leftover, less-than-crackly tofu chicherones are excellent additions to soups, where they immediately soften into silky, noodle-like morsels. Because they've been toasted in oil, they're especially delectable.

SRIRACHA POWDER

PREP TIME: 2 MINUTES | DRYING AND COOLING TIME: 90 MINUTES | MAKES ABOUT 3 TABLESPOONS

Oh my! This is some good stuff. Of course you'll want to use it on chips, popcorn, eggs...and pancakes? Just about any paste-style chili sauce can be made into a spicy red chili powder. You can play around with Thai, Vietnamese, and Korean brands, but the cock of the walk is the bottle with the big rooster on it.

Exciting news! Use this same method to make Ketchup Powder for ketchup flavored potato chips. In fact, any thick sauce can be dried to powder form, such as your favorite steak sauce, or terriaki, hoisin, and oyster sauce. A food dehydrator does a nearly perfect job at powder-making.

INGREDIENTS

¼ cup (2 ounces) Sriracha chili sauce, or any sauce
1 teaspoon fine salt, optional

METHOD

☐ Preheat the oven to 200°F and position an oven rack in the center.

☐ Line a baking sheet with parchment paper or a silicone baking mat.

☐ Use a rubber spatula or an offset cake spatula to spread the chili sauce across the sheet in a thin, even layer.

☐ Bake the sauce for about 30 minutes, turn the baking sheet, and continue baking it until it's dry and the edges flake easily with a fork—for about 30 to 40 more minutes.

☐ Allow the dried sauce to cool completely on the baking sheet for 20 to 30 minutes—it will continue to dry as it cools. Use a spatula to loosen and peel away the dried sheet and then transfer the pieces to a spice grinder or a sturdy, sealable plastic bag and use your fingers to grind it to a powder. This stuff is HOT, so don't get it in your eyes. Store Sriracha Powder in an airtight container.

SPICE TIP: Adding 1 teaspoon of fine salt, such as sea salt, helps to prevent the powder from caking.

DEHYDRATOR METHOD

☐ Cover a dehydrator tray with a non-stick liner or parchment paper. Use a rubber spatula or offset cake spatula to spread the mixture across the sheet in a thin, even layer.

☐ Dehydrate the mixture at 145°F for 3 to 6 hours. The length of time will depend on the model of your dehydrator and the humidity.

BAKED
CHARCUTERIE SAMPLER
PREP TIME: 5 MINUTES | BAKING TIME: 20 MINUTES | MAKES ABOUT 4 SERVINGS

With the increasing popularity of cured meats and sausages and the recent focus on the craft of drying and smoking them, more and more restaurants are offering charcuterie plates from local makers and from around the world. These salumi samplers are fun ways to compare flavors and textures.

Here's another take on the idea—in chip form: a spread of toothsome meats. Chips being a finger food, there's no need for crackers or bread, making this spread a paleo-perfect nosh. Here's how to set it up. Prepare three or more kinds of chips to fan across a cutting board or platter. For contrast, include un-chipped versions of some sausages. Drop in a few other nibbles—goat cheese, pickles, radishes—and set off the spread with the perfect condiment, Pickled Mustard Seeds (the recipe follows on page 136).

HUNTING-GATHERING

Just about any firm meat or sausage can be made into chips. At the deli counter, choose dense ham, beef, or turkey that's been pressed to hold together when sliced. Corned beef and pastrami may be too loose and stringy when cut to work as chips. You should also avoid soft and creamy sausages like bologna or liverwurst. Tell the deli person you want very thin slices—about 1/16 inch thick if you can specify—but not shaved so thin that the slices fall apart.

You'll find lots of choices in the packaged deli meats section too. Just be wary of anything described as shaved—make sure the meat isn't too thin. Whole, firm sausages are great options. Slice the fat ones like salami in rounds and the thinner ones like pepperoni in elongated diagonals.

MEATS FOR CHIPS

DELI MEAT
Smoked and honey-cured ham
Roast beef
Turkey breast
Pastrami

CURED MEAT
Prosciutto
Capocolla
Speck
Country ham

CURED SAUSAGE
Salami—cotto, genoa, and hard
Sopressata
Summer sausage
Pepperoni
Dry-aged chorizo

INGREDIENTS

8 ounces of thinly sliced deli meat, cured meat, or dry sausage

METHOD

☐ Preheat the oven to 350°F, with racks positioned in the upper and lower thirds

☐ Line two rimmed baking sheets with parchment paper or silicone baking mats.

☐ If your meat isn't pre-sliced, use your sharpest knife to cut thin and even slices that are not more than 1/16 inch thick. You may want to divide large slices into smaller pieces. Keep in mind that some meats shrink more than others in the oven, so you may need to experiment.

☐ Fill the baking sheets with slices, arranging the meat in single layers. Set aside the remaining slices for the next batch.

☐ Bake the slices for about 5 minutes, then check their progress. Flip the chips and turn the baking sheets, sending them back to opposite racks in the oven.

☐ Continue baking until the chips are dry and crisp. In most cases, the chips should be ready in another 5 to 10 minutes, but some meats and thicker slices may take longer. Keep a close watch on the chips. They're done when they begin to curl and brown slightly around the edges.

NOTE: Some meats tend to curl a lot. If that's the case for you, then flip and flatten the slices every 2 or 3 minutes.

☐ Transfer the chips to a paper towel-lined baking sheet or wire cooling rack. Note that meat chips, especially those made from sausage, will get crisper after 5 or 10 minutes out of the oven.

☐ Allow the chips to cool completely before sealing them in an airtight container. They can be stored in the refrigerator for about a week. To re-fresh and re-crisp cold or softened chips, warm them in a 300°F oven for about 5 minutes.

Embracing the Meat Chip

Once they're baked and dried into chips, meat and sausages become flavor bombs! Serve them alongside sandwiches, soups, and salads, or as the unique ingredient in recipes. Here are some ideas to springboard your own brilliant combinations.

AS APPETIZER
Salami chips spread across a platter, dotted with crumbled feta cheese, sprinkled with pickled red onions, and topped with fresh basil

Smoked turkey-breast chips plated in a single layer, topped with diced tomato, avocado, and radish sprouts—lightly drizzled with honey-mustard dressing

Roast beef chips dotted with horse-radish cream, baby arugula, and pickled red onions

AS INGREDIENT
Pepperoni chips in a hearty romaine, cucumber, onion, and tomato salad—tossed with tart and garlicky vinaigrette

Smoked-salmon chips tucked into cucumber-cream cheese sandwiches

Capocolla chips tossed with roasted asparagus, sprinkled with freshly squeezed lemon

AS SIDE
Hickory-smoked ham chips piled beside split-pea soup for dipping and dunking

Country ham chips banking an iceberg wedge salad, everything drizzled with chunky blue cheese dressing

PICKLED MUSTARD SEEDS

SOAKING TIME: 1 HOUR OR OVERNIGHT

COOKING TIME: 30 MINUTES | COOLING TIME: 1 HOUR

MAKES ABOUT 2 1/2 CUPS

This is a recipe I developed for my friend Ashley English (see her Baked Ras el Hanout Apple Chips recipe on page 127) for a mustard-making blog post she created for DesignSponge.com. Pickled mustard seeds are a versatile condiment and dip. Drizzle them over Fried Rainbow Beets (page 71) and appoint them as the dip to stand strong with Charcuterie Chips.

The little round seeds stay intact throughout the cooking process, so every single orb is a delightful flavor bomb in your mouth. Pickled mustard seeds are also an exciting pantry ingredient that can be added to salads, dressings, and gravies and used to spike the favor of other dips. The recipe makes enough to cover you for dipping, plus some extra for jazzing up the good things you create in the kitchen.

INGREDIENTS

1 cup (8 ounces) yellow mustard seeds, rinsed and drained

1 1/2 cups apple-cider or white-wine vinegar

1 teaspoon kosher salt

2 tablespoons honey

2 teaspoons turmeric

1/3-1/2 cup additional vinegar

METHOD

☐ Place the drained mustard seeds in a medium, non-reactive saucepan and add the vinegar and salt. Allow the seeds to soak uncovered at room temperature for at least 1 hour—overnight is better.

NOTE: Mustard is spiciest when it takes in cool liquid to become hydrated. Once heated, that aromatic mustard zing is locked in. That's why it's ideal for the seeds to soak in as much liquid as possible while they're cool.

☐ Add the honey and turmeric to the hydrated seeds and move the saucepan to the stovetop. Over medium heat, bring the mixture to a simmer and stir it with a wooden spoon, scraping the sides and bottom of the pan to prevent sticking. The mixture will bubble and sputter like polenta or grits, so constant stirring is important. Cook it for about 20 minutes.

☐ Remove the mustard from the heat and allow it to cool to room temperature, uncovered, for about 1 hour. The mixture will become thicker and denser as it cools.

☐ Stir in 1/3 to 1/2 cup more vinegar to thin the mixture and to freshen its flavor. Check the seasoning and add more salt, honey, or turmeric, if you like. Serve the dip immediately. It can be stored in glass jars in the refrigerator for up to a year.

NOTE: The mustard seeds will continue to absorb liquid for weeks. If the mixture becomes too dense, simply stir in a little more vinegar.

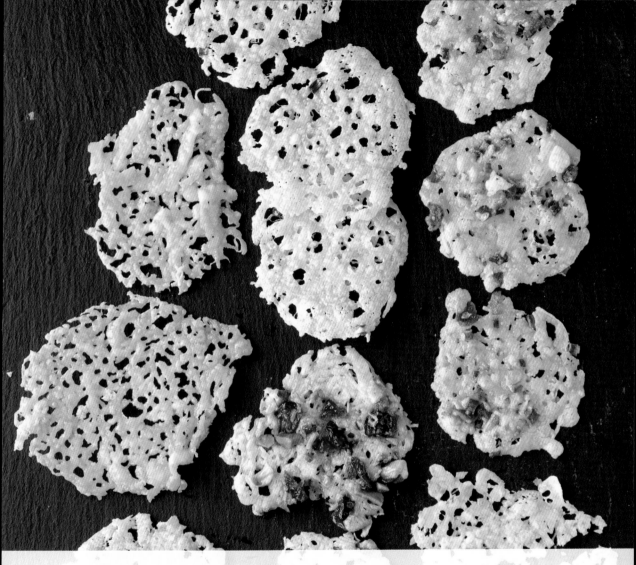

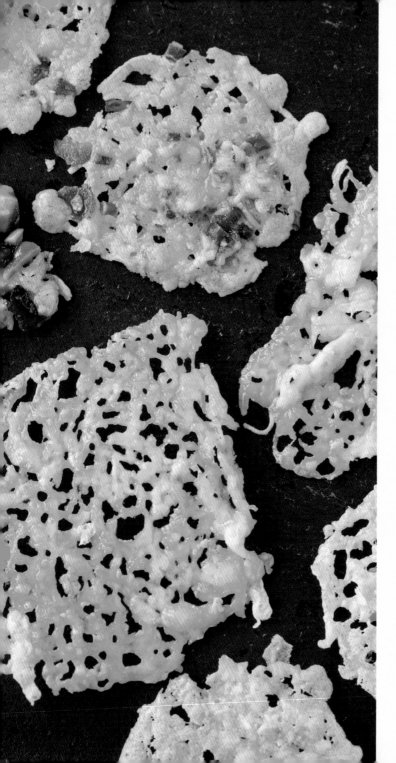

Classic *frico croccante* (loose translation: crisply fried cheese) comes from Italy's Friuli-Venezia Giulia region, where it's typically made with Montasio cheese. Frico-making is a fun trick. Into the oven go mounds of grated cheese; out comes lacy chips. Without a doubt, it's the simplest chip in the world to make.

Such a simple formula is wide open for improvisation. All manner of herbs, spices, and tasty tidbits can be bound up within the lacy net of cheese. Choose one or more of the inclusions listed—whatever you're in the mood for. How much to add is your call as well.

THE FRICO EXPERIENCE

Since it's all about the richness of cheese, frico begs to be paired with wine. Frico wafers can be dipped into or dotted with a velvety fig or tart cherry preserve. Frico chips are a wow addition to salads, and when you're down to the dregs, frico crumbles are fantastic over creamy soups and mashed potatoes!

HUNTING-GATHERING

Hard, grainy cheeses make the crispest, most flavorful frico. If you can't find Montasio, use Parmesan, Pecorino, Grana Padano, Asiago, or Mexican Cotija to capture their nutty flavor and edgy bite. Long-aged, flavorful varieties of Gouda, Manchego, Gruyère, and cheddar also make fantastic frico.

INGREDIENTS

8 ounces hard, flavorful cheese
1/2 teaspoon all-purpose flour (substitute
    potato or rice flour)
    Inclusions, optional

INCLUSIONS

Coarsely ground pepper—black, green, or white
Red pepper flakes, ground cayenne pepper,
    or smoked paprika
Whole cumin, fennel, caraway, or anise seeds
Dried delicate herbs—tarragon, basil, or chervil
Fresh herbs—rosemary, thyme, chives, or marjoram
Chopped pistachios, pecans, or black walnuts
Chopped dried cherries, cranberries, or candied
    citrus peel
Grated lemon or orange zest
Homemade bacon bits
Finely minced garlic

COMBINATIONS

Manchego with pistachio halves and diced
    dried cherries
Asiago with pickled green peppercorns (blotted dry)
Cheddar with chopped black walnuts
Gruyère with minced chives and bacon bits

CHIP TIP: **Keep moist inclusions to a minimum
and carefully dry pickled ingredients. Too much
moisture in the mix prevents frico from turning
crisp and delectable.**

METHOD

☐ Preheat the oven to 375°F, with the racks
positioned in the upper and lower thirds.

☐ Line two rimmed baking sheets with
parchment paper or silicone baking mats.

☐ Shred the cheese using the medium or small
holes of a grater. Note: For lacy frico, don't shred
the cheese too fine and don't use microplanes
that make powdery gratings.

☐ In a mixing bowl, add the grated cheese, flour,
and inclusions, if using. Toss gently until the
flour adheres evenly to the cheese.

☐ Drop about 2-teaspoon size mounds of the
cheese onto the baking sheets, spaced about
3 inches apart.

☐ Bake the frico until it's slightly colored and
toasty around the edges—10 to 15 minutes for most
cheeses. Some cheeses and inclusions may require
more time. Watch closely as the chips cook. Don't
allow them to become too brown. Use a spatula to
carefully remove the ones that get done first.

☐ Remove the chips from the oven and let them
cool and solidify for 2 or 3 minutes before handling.
Gently transfer them to a paper towel-lined surface
to pull away the oil. Allow the frico to cool
completely (for 15 to 20 minutes) before serving.

CHIP TIP: **When frico first comes out of the oven, it's
very pliable, and you can curl it. You can also turn the
flexible chips into little dip holders by draping them
over small bowls or shot glasses.**

☐ If you aren't serving the frico immediately,
leave the chips uncovered for at least 1 hour before
layering them between waxed paper and storing
them in an airtight container. Frico will keep for
about 2 days at room temperature and about
1 week refrigerated.

Tortilla chips made an amazing rise to the top. Since taking off in the 1970s, they're second only to potato chips. Every tortilla chip starts with a tortilla—one of the least expensive prepared foods on earth. A batch of homemade tortilla chips costs pennies to make, and homemade definitely tastes better than store bought. If you're a hardboiled DIY-er, go the extra step and craft your own tortillas!

~ BAKED ~

CHILI LIME CORN

PREP TIME: 10 MINUTES | COOKING TIME: 15 MINUTES

MAKES 60 CHIPS

For this recipe, tortilla wedges get tossed with lime zest, lime juice, and olive oil. Fresh and zippy! Use flour tortillas instead of corn for a lighter-flavored chip.

HUNTING-GATHERING
The freshest and best tortillas are found in tortillerias and Latin markets. In the supermarket, many brands are sold at room temperature, and others are refrigerated. Temperature doesn't matter. Some tortillas are thicker than others. Honduran- and Guatemalan-style tortillas are twice as thick as a typical tortilla and slightly fluffy. They make sturdy, cracker-like chips.

INGREDIENTS

    Cooking spray or oil for baking sheets
10 (5 or 6-inch) corn tortillas
2 tablespoons olive oil
1 tablespoon freshly squeezed lime juice
2 teaspoons grated lime zest (about 1 lime)
    Hint: grate the zest before juicing the lime
1 teaspoon chili powder
    teaspoon kosher salt
1/2 teaspoon garlic powder
1/8 teaspoon citric or ascorbic acid, optional
    More salt for seasoning

Ascendency of an Icon: A Brief history of the Tortilla Chip

The wedge-shaped chip we know and love was born around 1950 at the El Zarpe Tortilla Factory in Los Angles. To reclaim the imperfect tortillas that their newly installed automated tortilla machines rejected, Rebecca Webb Carranza and her husband cut the cast-offs into triangles, fried them, and sold them as snack chips for a dime a bag in their Mexican delicatessen. By the 1960s, the Carranza's "Tort Chips" had become their main product. The popularity of the chips spread throughout California, and other brands showed up that were distributed nationwide. Doritos debuted their "Taco Chips" in 1966. By the mid 70s, tortilla chips had knocked corn chips off the top of the chip pile.

METHOD

❏ Preheat the oven to 375°F, with the racks positioned in the upper and lower thirds.

❏ Spray or wipe two rimmed baking sheets with a light coating of oil.

☐ Slice the tortillas into 6 wedges, or 8 if you prefer—your call.

☐ In a large mixing bowl, combine the oil, lime juice, lime zest, chili powder, salt, garlic powder, and citric acid, if using.

☐ Gently toss the wedges in the mixture until they're well coated. Work quickly so they don't break or fall apart.

☐ Divide the wedges between the baking sheets and spread them out in single layers.

☐ Bake for 10 minutes and flip the slices—careful, they may be fragile at first. Turn the baking sheets, switch their positions in the oven, and continue baking until the chips are crisp and light golden-brown—for another 5 to 10 minutes. Watch the chips closely and stir them around if they're cooking unevenly. They can go from toasty to charred in seconds toward the end.

☐ Sprinkle the chips with more salt, if you like. To store, allow them to cool completely. They'll keep in an airtight container for about 5 days. If the chips get soft, re-crisp them in a 300°F oven for 4 or 5 minutes.

FRIED

FAUX-RITOS STYLE CORN

PREP TIME: 15 MINUTES | COOKING TIME: 20 MINUTES | MAKES 60 CHIPS

Whether you stand up for flavor science or rail against it, you have to agree that Doritos Nacho Brand chips posses a flavor formula that makes the snacking masses consume whole bags in one sitting, all the way down to the last crumb. Or maybe that's just me.

You don't need a laboratory to create your own addictive nacho-flavored chips. The following formula is composed of basic pantry spices. Note that just about every ingredient pings somewhere on the umami scale.

INGREDIENTS

10 (5 to 6-inch) corn tortillas
3 or more tablespoons corn, canola, or vegetable oil
   Cooking spray or oil for baking sheets
6 tablespoons ($^{1}/_{3}$ cup) Nacho-Flavor Powder, recipe follows

METHOD

☐ Before you start, gather a large strainer or a handled colander fitted over a bowl to catch oil; a medium-size, sturdy paper bag for shaking the seasoning; and two large baking sheets to cool and dry the chips.

☐ Pour about $1^{1}/_{2}$ inches of oil into a wide, heavy pot, deep skillet, or wok. Leave 2 inches of headspace above the oil or 3 inches of rim around the wok. Attach a cooking thermometer and bring the oil to 350°F over medium-high heat.

☐ Working in stacks of 3 or 4, slice the tortillas into 6 wedges.

☐ Carefully drop some of the wedges into the oil without crowding the pot. (I did mine in a wok in 4 batches.) Use a slotted spoon or spider to move and turn the chips in the oil until they begin to turn golden-brown around the edges—in about 1 or 2 minutes. Watch the chips closely and don't let them get too dark.

☐ Scoop the chips into the strainer and let some oil drip into the bowl while you scoop 4 teaspoons of Nacho-Flavor Powder into the paper bag. Dump the

NACHO-FLAVOR POWDER

MAKES 6 TABLESPOONS (ABOUT 1/3 CUP)

This zesty seasoning is good on just about everything. Try it on kale or zucchini chips, or venture outside the chip kingdom and sprinkle it on popcorn, grilled-cheese sandwiches, and roast corn on the cob. Or dip in and eat it straight, but double the recipe if you plan to do a lot of that.

INGREDIENTS

- 2 tablespoons nutritional yeast
- 1 tablespoon Parmesan and Romano cheese (the boxed kind)
- 2 teaspoons buttermilk powder, sour cream powder, or cheese powder (see Cheese Flavorings, page 23)
- 2 teaspoons chili powder
- 1 teaspoon sweet or hot paprika (bright red is best)
- 1 teaspoon table salt or fine sea salt
- 1 teaspoon brown sugar
- 1/2 teaspoon ground cumin
- 1/2 teaspoon garlic powder
- 1/2 teaspoon dry mustard
- 1/2 teaspoon onion powder
- 1/8 teaspoon ascorbic or citric acid
- 1/8 teaspoon cayenne powder, or to taste

METHOD

☐ Combine all of the ingredients in a food mill or blender and pulse for 3 or 4 seconds, until the ingredients are blended into an even-textured powder. Store the powder in an airtight container in the refrigerator, and it'll be good for about 2 months.

chips in the bag and shake, gently turning the bag upside down a couple of times to coat the chips. Dump them onto a baking sheet to cool.

☐ Continue to fry the remaining wedges, keeping the oil at 350°F, making room on the baking sheets for the next batch, and allowing the chips to drain a few seconds before shaking them with the seasoning.

☐ To store, allow the chips to cool completely before transferring them to an airtight container. They'll keep at room temperature for about a week. But they won't last that long.

CINNAMON SOPAPILLA CHIPS

PREP TIME: 5 MINUTES | COOKING TIME: 20 MINUTES | MAKES 30 CHIPS

Here's an easy interpretation of New Mexico's sticky, sweet sopapillas using flour tortillas. These are some incredible dessert chips. Unlike traditional sopapillas, which are softer and puffier, these are sturdy—perfect for scooping up ice cream. I suggest vanilla or pineapple. But chocolate would be *más excelente* too. Oh, you decide.

INGREDIENTS

> 5 (8 to 10-inch) flour tortillas
> Neutral oil for frying

SEASONING
> 1/4 cup light brown sugar
> 1/4 cup confectioner's sugar
> 2 teaspoons cinnamon

METHOD

☐ Before you start, gather a large strainer or handled colander that can be fitted over a bowl to catch the oil; a medium-sized, sturdy paper bag for shaking the seasoning; and one large baking sheet for cooling and drying the chips. Arrange these near your cooktop.

☐ In a small bowl, combine the brown sugar, confectioner's sugar, and cinnamon. Set the mixture near the paper bag.

☐ Pour about 1 1/2 inches of oil into a wide, heavy pot, deep skillet, or wok. Leave 2 inches of headspace above the oil or 3 inches of rim around the wok. Attach a cooking thermometer and bring the oil to 350°F over medium-high heat.

☐ Working in stacks of 3 or 4, slice the tortillas into 6 wedges.

☐ Carefully drop some of the wedges into the oil without crowding the pot. (I did mine in a wok in 3 batches.) Use a slotted spoon or spider to move and turn the chips in the oil until they begin to turn golden-brown around the edges—in about 1 or 2 minutes. Watch the chips closely and don't let them get too dark.

☐ Scoop the chips into the strainer. Let some oil drip into the bowl while you scoop a portion of the seasoning mixture into the paper bag. While they're still hot, dump the chips in the bag and shake it, gently turning it upside down a couple of times to coat the chips. Dump them onto the baking sheet to cool.

☐ Continue to fry the remaining wedges, keeping the oil at 350°F and making room on the baking sheet for the next batch. Allow the chips to drain for a few seconds before shaking them with the seasoning.

☐ To store the chips, allow them to cool completely before transferring them to an airtight container. They'll keep at room temperature for about a week.

SERVING SUGGESTIONS

■ Drizzle the chips with honey or chocolate syrup

■ Tuck them into individual bowls of ice cream

■ Serve them with guacamole sweetened with honey

BAGELS

Are you the one who digs through the snack mix to pick out the fat bagel chips? Thought so. Their super-rich flavor is irresistible. That's because the bagels are sponges that absorb more of the flavoring than anything else in the bag. So let's use that sponge effect to make a no-picking-necessary snack.

Making bagel chips is a lot like making croutons. As with croutons, there's some butter or oil involved, plus some seasonings. An infinite range of flavor blends can be devised. That said, I limited each of these blends to nine ingredients—you need not be so disciplined. Go kitchen sink if you like.

I usually make C-shaped chips because they're easier to slice, and the size is good for snacking. But the shape of big rounds, horizontally cut, looks good on an appetizer spread, and folks like to break them up. Then there are mini bagels. I personally don't understand them. (Why miniature bagels?) But they do make cute little O-shaped chips that are very similar to those in the snack mix.

INGREDIENTS

3-4 plain bagels, preferably unsplit
Good-quality cooking spray or oil mister
Seasoning blend, choose from the recipes
on page 148

METHOD

☐ Preheat the oven to 350°F, with the racks positioned in the upper and lower thirds.

☐ Line two (or more if your oven has room) rimmed baking pans with silicone baking mats or parchment paper.

☐ In a small bowl (or bowls, if you're making other flavors), combine the ingredients for the seasoning marinade and set it aside.

☐ For oval chips, lay the bagels flat and cut them lengthwise into thin slices—between $1/8$ and $3/16$ inch thick (as thick as 2 or 3 stacked quarters). For C-shapes, halve the bagels lengthwise and place the "rainbows" cut-side down for easy cutting. For mini bagels, cut horizontal slices to make O-shaped chips.

CHIP TIP: Slightly frozen bagels are way easier to cut. Put them in the freezer for 30 to 40 minutes before preparing the chips

☐ Arrange the slices on the baking sheets in a single layer (you may need to work in batches) and give them a generous hit of cooking spray.

☐ Flip the slices and apply the seasoning blend. For the Party Mix Classic and Sweet Cinnamon Spice toppings, brush and dab the mixture on the pieces. For the Sour Cream & Onion, spread the mixture with a small spatula. Sprinkle the pieces with sugar or salt, according to each seasoning blend recipe.

☐ Bake for 10 minutes, then flip the slices. Return the baking sheets to the oven on opposite racks. Bake for another 5 minutes, flip the pieces again, and turn the pans again. Return the chips to the oven and let them bake until they're golden-brown and very crisp, like hard toast. This may take an extra 5 to 10 minutes, depending on how thick you sliced the bagels and how moist they are. Keep a close watch on the chips, as the oil accelerates the browning process.

NOTE: Sour Cream & Onion chips may remain a little soft in their centers. That's okay. They'll taste all the better for it.

☐ Remove the chips from the baking sheets and let them cool and dry in a single layer for 10 or more minutes. They'll get crisper as they cool. Allow them to sit out for 1 hour before putting them in a closed container.

❑ You can store bagel chips in an airtight container at room temperature for about 4 days. Refrigerated, they'll be good for a week or more.

BONUS! These chips improve with age. The Party Mix Classic and Sour Cream & Onion ones are most amazing after a day or two.

SEASONING BLENDS

PARTY MIX CLASSIC

  3 tablespoons butter, melted
  2 tablespoons olive oil
  4 teaspoons Worcestershire sauce
$1/2$ teaspoon cider vinegar
$1/2$ teaspoon onion powder
$1/2$ teaspoon freshly ground black pepper
$1/4$ teaspoon garlic powder, or $1/2$ teaspoon fresh grated garlic
$1/4$ teaspoon paprika
   Salt for sprinkling

Variation: Make it buffalo style by adding 1–2 teaspoons pepper sauce

SWEET CINNAMON SPICE

  4 tablespoons butter, melted
  1 tablespoon oil, walnut oil would be nice
$1/2$ teaspoon pure vanilla extract
  2 tablepoons brown sugar
$3/4$ teaspoon ground cinnamon
$1/4$ teaspoon ground dried ginger
$1/8$ teaspoon freshly ground nutmeg
1-2 tablespoons granulated sugar for sprinkling

SOUR CREAM & ONION

$1/4$ cup neutral-flavored oil
  2 tablespoons cream cheese, melted
  1 tablespoon finely minced chives or scallion greens
  2 teaspoons finely grated onion
  2 teaspoons distilled (white) vinegar
$3/4$ teaspoon onion powder
   Salt for sprinkling

IONIAN PITA CHIPS WITH CAESAR'S DIP

PREP TIME: 15 MINUTES | **BAKING TIME:** 15 MINUTES | **MAKES 24–32 CHIPS**

The basic formula for making pita chips is just a degree more complicated than the one for making homemade ice cubes: Brush pita wedges with oil. Toast. Add seasonings and embellishments at will. Within a few minutes you have tasty chips!

Give these simple chips an Imperial Upgrade by serving them with the Caesar's Dip and feta toppings that follow. For another stately pairing, serve the chips with Winnie Abramson's Cool Hummus Dip on page 65.

HUNTING-GATHERING
Look for pocket pitas that easily separate into two layers.

INGREDIENTS

    Cooking spray or oil for coating
 1 teaspoon fresh oregano, finely chopped
    (^{1}/$_2$ teaspoon dried)
 1 teaspoon fresh rosemary, finely chopped
    (^{1}/$_2$ teaspoon dried)
 1 teaspoon fresh thyme, freshly chopped
    (^{1}/$_2$ teaspoon dried)
 ^{1}/$_2$ teaspoon course-ground black pepper
 ^{1}/$_2$ teaspoon kosher salt
 ^{1}/$_2$ teaspoon red pepper flakes, optional
 ^{1}/$_2$ cup extra-virgin olive oil
 1 teaspoon (2 cloves) freshly grated or
    pressed garlic
 4 loaves of pita bread
    Fresh rosemary, coarsely chopped, optional

METHOD

☐ Preheat the oven to 350°F, with the racks positioned in the upper and lower thirds.

☐ Spray or lightly oil two rimmed baking sheets.

☐ In a small bowl combine the oregano, rosemary, thyme, black pepper, salt, and red pepper, if using. Set the seasoning blend aside.

☐ In another bowl, combine the olive oil and garlic.

☐ Stack the pitas and cut them into 6 or 8 wedges. Carefully peel apart the wedges and arrange them in a single layer on the baking sheets with their exterior (smoother) sides up. Lightly brush the pieces with some of the oil, flip them, and generously brush the interior (rougher) sides with the remaining oil. Sprinkle with the seasoning blend.

☐ Bake the pita pieces for 10 minutes and then flip them. Turn the baking sheets and switch their positions in the oven.

☐ Continue baking until the chips turn golden-brown, for about 5 to 10 minutes more. Your time may vary, so watch the chips closely and remove the ones that finish first. When they're done, they'll curl a little, be a bit toasty, and feel light.

☐ Serve the chips with Caesar's Dip (see opposite), and sprinkled with fresh rosemary, if you like.

☐ If you don't eat the chips immediately, allow them to cool and dry completely—for at least 30 minutes—before transferring them to an airtight container. They can be stored at room temperature for about a week.

VARIATIONS:

▉ Change up the way you use the Caesar's Dip. Use it to replace some of the olive oil in the recipe.

▉ When you flip the chips, sprinkle them with crumbled feta cheese.

CAESAR'S DIP

MAKES ABOUT ½ CUP

All hail the triumvirate of garlic, anchovy, and olive oil! It's the eternal kitchen combo. This lemon-spiked iteration makes a supremely civilized dip. Or try it drizzled over a platter of kettle-style potato chips. Oh, and it's a darned good salad dressing in its own right.

INGREDIENTS

- ½ teaspoon (1 clove) finely chopped garlic
- 3-4 anchovy fillets, finely chopped
- ¼ teaspoon kosher salt
- ⅓ cup extra-virgin olive oil
- 2 tablespoons Dijon mustard
- ¼ teaspoon grated lemon zest
- ¼ teaspoon freshly ground black pepper
- ¼ teaspoon sugar
- ¼ teaspoon Worcestershire sauce
- 1 tablespoon freshly squeezed lemon juice

METHOD

☐ Lay the chopped garlic and anchovies near the edge of your cutting surface, and sprinkle them with the salt. Chop everthing very fine, then, with the side of the knife blade, mash the mixture together until you have a fine paste.

☐ In a mixing bowl, combine the anchovy-garlic paste, Dijon mustard, lemon zest, pepper, sugar, and Worcestershire sauce. Whisk in the olive oil, adding it in a slow and steady stream so that the mixture emulsifies. Whisk in the lemon juice and blend until the dip becomes lighter.

WONTONS

Here's another simple, simple, simple chip shortcut. You've surely succumbed to the tasty temptation of fried wonton chips! Especially the ones in the bag of Chinese takeout that never make it to the table. Wontons have tons of potential as a snack chip thanks to premade wonton wrappers—the perfect palette for lots of creativity.

~ BAKED ~

BAKED JAPANESE WASABI OR MAYAN SWEET

PREP TIME: 15 MINUTES | COOKING TIME: 15 MINUTES

MAKES 48 CHIPS

Here's a way to really layer on the flavors. Start out by coating the wontons with a penetrating flavor wash and then press toppings into their surface. Two variations offer savory and sweet options. The Japanese Wasabi version is my favorite—I more than double the wasabi when I make them. The Mayan Sweet chips turn into an out-of-the-ordinary dessert when paired with ice cream and the Azteca Chocolate-Chili Dip on page 110.

HUNTING-GATHERING

Furikake is a flaky Japanese condiment that's sprinkled over rice, soups, and lots of other things. It's available in blends ranging from mild to hot. The main ingredients in furikake are dried seaweed, dried fish (bonito), salt, sugar, and sesame seeds. You can find it at Asian grocery stores and in the foreign food section of many grocery stores.

INGREDIENTS

24 (4 x 4) wonton wrappers
 Cooking spray or oil for misting

FLAVOR WASHES

JAPANESE WASABI
 1 medium egg, well beaten
 1 tablespoon wasabi paste (or 2 teaspoons powdered plus 1 teaspoon water)
 1 teaspoon granulated sugar
 1 teaspoon kosher salt
 1/2 teaspoon toasted sesame oil
 Topping: 2 tablespoons furikake seasoning (see Hunting-Gathering) (substitute sesame seeds)

MAYAN SWEET
 3 tablespoons butter, melted
 1/2 teaspoon vanilla extract
 1 tablespoon brown sugar
 1 teaspoon ground cinnamon
 Topping: 2 tablespoons toasted sesame seeds
 1 tablespoon granulated sugar, for sprinkling after applying the topping

METHOD

❑ Preheat the oven to 375°F, with the racks positioned in the upper and lower thirds.

❑ Line two rimmed baking sheets with parchment paper or silicone baking mats.

❑ Choose a flavor wash from the list. Combine its ingredients in a small bowl and measure out the topping in another bowl. Set the bowls aside.

❑ Working in stacks of 4, divide the wontons into triangles or cut them lengthwise into thirds to make chip strips.

☐ Arrange the wonton pieces closely on the baking sheets. Spray or mist them with oil and flip the pieces. Brush the other side with one of the flavor washes. Sprinkle on the topping and gently press it into the surface of the wontons with a rolling pin or the flat bottom of a glass. For the Mayan Sweet chips, sprinkle the wontons with the granulated sugar after pressing in the topping.

NOTE: There may be more Japanese Wasabi wash than you need.

☐ Bake the pieces for 7 minutes, then turn the baking pans and trade out their positions in the oven. Continue to bake the chips until they're golden-brown around the edges and begin to curl a bit—for another 5 to 8 minutes, depending on the flavor wash.

☐ The chips will get crisper as they cool, especially the Mayan Sweet chips. Don't stack the chips until they're completely cool, or they may soften.

☐ Let the chips cool and dry completely—for at least 30 minutes—before sealing them in an airtight container for storage. You can store them at room temperature for about a week. If they get soft, reheat them in a 350°F oven for 3 or 4 minutes.

~ FRIED ~

FRIED SWEET AND SAVORY WONTON

PREP TIME: 5 MINUTES | FRYING TIME: 10 MINUTES | MAKES 24 CHIPS | BAKING TIME: 5–10 MINUTES

The process here is basic as it gets—you cut some wontons in half, fry them up, and add seasoning. That's all you need to do to make tasty chips, and there are so many great seasoning blends in the book to dust on them.

Going a step further—and ramping up the flavor—this sweet-and-savory topping gets melted onto the chips after a quick pass through the oven. The sugar and yeast take hold to create a delightful crunch. You can also bake on a topping of Parmesan cheese and herbs. If fast and simple is your aim, then sprinkle the topping on each batch of chips as they come out of the oil. Just do it quickly while the surface of the chips is still glistening so that the seasoning sticks.

INGREDIENTS

  2 tablespoons confectioner's sugar
  2 tablespoons sesame seeds
  1 teaspoon nutritional yeast
  $1/2$ teaspoon kosher salt or a chunky sea salt
  $1/8$ teaspoon citric or ascorbic acid, optional
  12 (4 x 4) wonton wrappers
     Oil for frying
     Fine sea salt

METHOD

☐ Line two rimmed baking sheets with silicone baking mats or parchment paper and preheat the oven to 350°F.

☐ In a small bowl, combine the sugar, sesame seeds, nutritional yeast, salt, and citric or ascorbic acid, if using.

☐ Pour 1 to $1/2$ inches of oil into a heavy, deep pot or wok, leaving at least 2 inches of headspace above the oil or 3 inches of rim around the wok. Attach a cooking thermometer and bring the oil to 350°F over high heat.

☐ Working in stacks of 4, cut the wonton wrappers in half diagonally to make triangles.

☐ Drop 5 or 6 of the triangles into the hot oil. They cook in seconds, so don't do too many at a time. Use a slotted spoon or spider to move and turn the chips in the oil until they're barely golden—for 5 to 10 seconds. Make sure you don't overcook them, because they'll be spending some time in the oven next.

☐ Transfer the chips directly to the baking sheets and continue to fry the remaining wedges, keeping the oil at 350°F.

☐ When they chips are done, spread them out evenly on the baking sheets. Sprinkle them with the seasoning blend, aiming for the center of each chip. Bake for 5 to 10 minutes, until the blend looks sealed to the surface, and the chips are a deep golden-brown. Let the chips cool on the baking sheets for 10 to 15 minutes before serving so that the topping can harden onto the surface.

☐ The chips should cool completely—for at least 30 minutes—before you seal them in an airtight container for storage. Store them at room temperature for about 4 days. If they get soft, reheat them in a 350°F oven for 3 or 4 minutes.

Editor: Linda Kopp
Art Director: Kristi Pfeffer
Photographer: Lynne Harty

ABOUT THE AUTHOR

During a long run as Senior Art Director at Lark Books in Asheville, North Carolina, Chris Bryant became the in-house food authority, using his knowledge of cooking and culinary trends to guide the development of Lark's food titles, including the *Homemade Living* Series, *Cake Ladies*, and *A Year of Pies*. Now Chris is a freelance food and photo stylist, recipe developer and tester, and cookbook writer. He's currently gearing up to launch extraslaw.com, his much–anticipated, long-delayed food blog. He is a member of the Southern Foodways Alliance, Slow Food USA, and Culinary Historians of Piedmont North Carolina. Chris and his husband, Skip, live in West Asheville in a house filled with Chris's cherished community, regional, and vintage cookbooks.

ACKNOWLEDGMENTS

I'll start with a hearty hip-hip-hooray and word of thanks to Linda Kopp, editor of *Chips*. It was Linda who decided the time was right for this book.

My endless gratitude goes to Nicole McConville, a good friend and the leader of Lark's Craft Your Life Team. Thank you, Nicole, for giving me the opportunity to run with a fun idea and write a cookbook.

I tip my hat to Lark editors Thom O'Hearn, for putting me out on a long leash to play with ideas, and Julie Hale, for seeing to it that my words and instructions make sense. And I send a big hug to Kathy Sheldon, author, editor, and friend, for her encouraging words and eagle-eyed final editing. Kathy, I'm so fortunate that you had a hand in this.

These beautifully designed pages came about thanks to the limitless creativity of Lark art director Kristi Pfeffer, who conjured up the exact book I was hoping for. Kristi, you are the best! I'm also indebted to genius photographer Lynne Harty, whose skill, talent, and artistic eye are awe-inspiring. Lynne, your photos bring this food to life.

Big thanks go to *Chips* recipe contributors Marissa Lippert, Todd Porter and Diane Cu, Winnie Abramson, Mark Owen, and Ashley English. You're my heroes. I was humbled by your enthusiasm and willingness to develop excellent recipes for this project. *Chips* is better for your presence.

And, finally, to my husband, Skip Wade, a good and patient man who endured the test-kitchen and dining room-turned-photo studio phases of this project: I raise a glass to three decades of shared adventures in food and eating. This book is dedicated to you. You get a batch of Nacho Kale Chips anytime you want.

INDEX

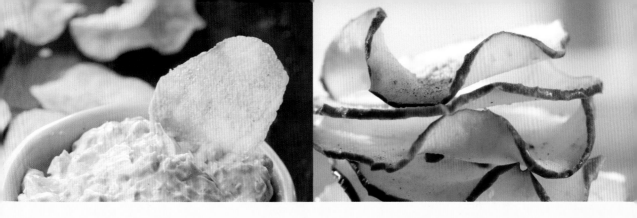